LOCALMOTION

HOW TECHNOLOGY IS PERSONALIZING THE GLOBAL MARKETPLACE

Alex Barseghian

LOCALMOTION

How Technology Is Personalizing the Global Marketplace

ISBN   978-1-5445-1211-2 *Paperback*
       978-1-5445-1212-9 *Ebook*

It is so hard to sum up a motto when there are many quotes that are applicable in many situations. For me, this book and my approach to life can be summed up by this: "If you can do something today, why wait until tomorrow?" I hope this book inspires you to take action today and helps you tackle LocalMotion.

This book is dedicated to my parents and extended family who supported me in all my endeavors, and to my wife, Lavinia, and sons, Andrew and James, who inspire me to make every day happen.

A special thanks to Michael Beckerman, Lou Clements, Terry Mathews, Brice Scheschuk, Kelly Shipman, Bill Tauscher, Kat Thomas, Ann Marie Tosoni, Bill Wignall, and countless others who helped me along this journey of LocalMotion.

CONTENTS

INTRODUCTION

THE LOCAL TREND

The global marketplace is at a tipping point. We're living in a time when technology is enabling individuals and communities to buy, sell, invest, and innovate in increasingly local ways. New and emerging ecommerce platforms are connecting local sellers with buyers across oceans and continents. The seller may be a wood-carver in Borneo or a weaver in Peru. The buyer may reside in Tahiti or Toronto. We are witnessing a convergence of technology and locally sourced products and services from Beijing to Banff.

The depth of smartphone penetration throughout the world has allowed for companies to become "individual smart." By knowing individual preferences and behavior, companies can better understand what to recommend and how to assist individuals in their daily activities, such as transportation, shopping, entertainment, and dining.

Who would have thought that individuals could put their homes online and rent directly to travelers until Airbnb came along? Or that smartphone apps would bring an Uber driver, a bottle of single malt Scotch, or a personal trainer to your door? Or that craft beer would outsell Budweiser? Or that McDonald's would be promoting locally sourced Filet-O-Fish?

The central force of local motion is around personalization and the adoption of technology to allow companies to individualize better and speak to the heart and mind of consumers. Artificial intelligence (AI) is the growing tool that will enable companies to target and engage with more relevance than ever before.

Companies that invest in understanding what their customers need and want are going to be far more successful in the future than those that don't. Businesses that clue in to our new "localmotion" marketplace will ride the new commercial wave. Those that don't will struggle to stay afloat.

INDIVIDUALS AND COMMUNITIES

In the new global marketplace, consumers have matured

and people are increasingly wary of the old corporate juggernauts. This became increasingly apparent in the wake of the Great Recession of 2008. The disruption to economies worldwide and the devastation to local Main Street businesses put people on notice that globalization had major drawbacks. Everyday people reacted with heightened awareness and cynicism about the machinations of the global economy, and a shift occurred in their thinking.

Instead of remaining complacent and detached from economic forces, individuals—also known as consumers and customers—began to assert their desire for a marketplace that is more responsive to people's needs. They wanted to be better served by goods and services, and the companies that provide them. They wanted to feel attached to things and have influence over the nature, selection, and quality of the goods and services they use at a local level.

As we'll explore more deeply in chapter 1, this change in thinking reached a tipping point in 2013. A new breed of entrepreneur began stepping up with innovative products and services, such as Airbnb and 3-D printing, that increasingly personalized the marketplace. It was exactly what people wanted, needed, and were demanding. The detachment from global economic forces that had existed before the Great Recession was giving way to new attachments at the local level for people with similar interests and needs.

This shift to local has evolved in stages. People don't change their spending all at once. Individual buying habits are shifting gradually, but increasingly, to more engagement with local sourcing of goods and services in an ever-widening economy.

TECHNOLOGY, THE GREAT DISRUPTOR

Driving the change is information technology (IT), AI, and digital applications that can personalize buying and product selection. Companies are beginning to understand that it's the individual, not industry, who is at the center of commerce. In our new age of connectivity, a new economy is shaping up to challenge the very definitions of what global and local mean.

IT has enabled innumerable startups, online commerce, and new ways of finding and securing venture capital. Community-based incubators have begun supporting inspiring new companies. Capital today is being raised in small amounts among individuals coming together in like-minded communities. Kernels of ideas are finding financial backers. Individuals are pooling money and "crowdfunding" new businesses headed by our new breed of inspired entrepreneurs.

What the internet has done is cut out the middlemen. We are living in an age of direct seller-to-buyer sales and a continually growing pantheon of platforms. Airbnb is facilitating individual-to-individual interaction and commerce. Amazon knows that if I'm a man buying diapers online, chances are certain I'm a new dad who needs a lot of other baby stuff.

Traditional chain stores such as Nordstrom and Family Dollar are doing market research in their stores by following Wi-Fi signals on our smartphones. In-store analytics are tracking customers while we shop. They want to know our shopping patterns, how we respond to displays, how long we spend looking and deciding.

Advancing innovation into the future is artificial intelligence. AI is increasingly shaping the culture of how individuals connect with products and services. Our new age of connectivity is enabling the internet of things (IoT), objects embedded with software that can be sensed and controlled remotely across a personalized network. AI can generate algorithms around an individual's buying tastes and behavior. AI is all about predictability, whether it's applied to driverless cars, climate control in our homes, our music apps, or our buying decisions online.

As we'll see in coming chapters, AI and the IoT are becoming determining factors in the success of companies. Those that understand and integrate leading-edge technology will better serve individuals and reap the rewards.

Industries and businesses from health-care systems to banks to car manufacturers to internet companies are all planning for growth around AI for one simple reason: AI makes it easier to know the individual consumer and to enable consumers to buy products and use services.

MACRO SHIFTS TO MICRO

The shift toward a local orientation is occurring globally at the macrolevel. In fact, the new macroeconomy is actually micro-oriented to local environments. Global companies that identify and connect to the local movement are mostly startups, such as Uber, Airbnb, and the robo-advisor Wealthsimple. Companies such as these, and the people behind them, are challenging the status quo. They understand the shift from macro to micro.

At the microlevel, size doesn't matter as much as it used to. Serving the individual can occur on a small scale. Our newest generations, millennials and Gen Z, are a worldwide cohort of individuals born into a world that is much more expensive, much more in debt, and overleveraged. They live in condensed urban environments in areas of mixed-use development. They are digital natives with new reference points for how they want to live, buy, and consume.

As you'll see in these pages, marketers can no longer rely

on old-school demographics that segment populations by age, gender, or other common reference points. IT is refining data collection to the individual. Netflix has displaced the Blockbusters of the world by offering choices personalized to individual tastes.

We are still only at the dawn of the mobile digital age. Retailers are only beginning to link brick-and-mortar sales to the digital potential of the IoT. It's an exciting time, a turbulent and disruptive time, which is why I'm writing this book.

THAT ELUSIVE SOMETHING

People today are looking for an elusive something, and that elusive something is authenticity. It's what localmotion is all about—finding personal and community connections in the things we do and the products we buy.

How we consume, where we invest, and whom we associate with online or in person are all converging in a global society of individuals finding value in community. It's where commerce is heading. The tangible value of goods sold is increasingly linked to who made it, how it was made, where it was made, and was the maker fairly compensated.

In our changing economic landscape, McDonald's will be under increasing strain to understand its customers and suppliers and give them something back. Online companies such as Amazon are already doing that. Amazon delivers on the customer first—both the individual and the community. When you're shopping on Amazon, you are provided with related suggestions based on your own buying preferences and those of others who've searched the same or similar merchandise. Amazon has learned to map, shape, and master what it means for a company to speak both to the individual and the community. Reviews by Amazon customers lend credibility to the buying experience. You can trust individual opinions weighed against the aggregate of an online buying community of sci-fi readers, cooks, or film buffs.

HOW I GOT HERE

I came to localmotion through my work with SambaConnects, a company I founded to connect local businesses with larger retail venues. It's based on a concept of Main Street shopping. SambaConnects embraces technology that helps small companies enter larger markets by bringing their gift cards to major retailers and by providing a technology platform that reduces the barrier to entry.

SambaConnects brings localized content to the mass market. It helps local businesses get a foot in the door of retail chains and large digital companies such as PayPal. At the same time, SambaConnects is an umbrella company for three other brands: Samba Days, WaySpa, and Life Experiences, which offer affordable gift experiences based in local areas that aren't far from home. They tap a need of people wanting to share their experiences with family and friends. There is an overall shift from gifting stuff to gifting experiences; we are well for increased relevancy.

YOUR LOCAL TOUR

Localmotion has caught on because it's where people want to go. It's where these pages will take you. I conceived this book as something of a tour of major changes afoot in how business is conducted locally and globally.

In the first part of the tour, we'll explore the remarkable shifts in the consumer landscape toward the individual. Across all industries from food to high tech, and in every corner of the world, the individual is becoming the center of a new localized economy.

In the tour's second part, you'll see how savvy businesses are embracing community to enable new forms of local consumerism. In the global marketplace, consumers are coming together in like-minded communities and making decisions about what they want to buy online and offline.

The third part of the tour explores leading-edge technology that has empowered the consumer and fueled the local movement. Without the internet, social media, apps, connectivity, mobile devices, and ecommerce, we would never have reached this extraordinary place in time.

So come along for the tour. You'll see how the new local paradigm is changing our present and our future. You'll learn how brands, startups, and corporate strategies are driving, adapting, or failing to adapt to the increasing power of localmotion.

THE INDIVIDUAL

Chapter 1

WHAT DOES LOCAL MEAN TO YOU?

The tectonic plates of commerce are shifting, and the world is moving toward a new consumer model. In this trend toward localmotion, individuals want to connect with goods, services, and ways of living that provide more meaning. They don't want the same old grind.

THE NEW CONSUMER MODEL

This change didn't happen overnight. Actually, it occurred in three phases. Take the coffee industry for example.

In the first phase of the coffee industry, grounds and instant coffees were mass produced by companies such as Maxwell House and Folgers. Coffee was percolated on stovetops and in big urns in diners. It was served piping hot with cream and sugar to taste, and almost any coffee grounds would do. As early as 1938, instant coffee was mass marketed by Nescafé. During phase one of our romance with coffee, individual tastes didn't matter very much. The coffee industry was all about marketing to the masses.

Then came Starbucks and phase two of the coffee industry. The new kid on the block introduced consumers to the European model of coffee houses with darker roasts, espressos, lattes, and Arabica beans. Starbucks offered a new taste and a different coffee experience. They introduced new choices and handcrafted coffee to the North American market.

Dunkin' Donuts never dreamed that people would pay $4 for coffee. Who would have thought that a Seattle coffee chain would move past the prepackaged Maxwell Houses of the world? But at Starbucks, people learned a whole new language of coffee. Starbucks succeeded by taking its brand to the individual and selling an entirely different coffee experience. Highly flavorful, dark roasts and handcrafted drinks became personal treats. People learned to order half-caf macchiato ventis with caramel.

Now that Starbucks has been around for a while, what's next?

The trend in localmotion continues to move the business community toward deeper personalization of goods and services. In phase three of the coffee industry, the consumer experience is becoming even more personalized. In this phase, the coffee shop experience is taking us back to our roots when neighbors knew each other better and business was local.

I call phase three "deep local." In this phase, your corner coffee shop is staffed by people who know you. It's the *Cheers* model, kind of like the old corner bar. Your neighborhood café doesn't need to ask your name or your order, because they already know it. Their coffee is roasted on the premises the very day you drink it. Ounce by ounce, it's brewed to your distinct taste preferences.

Starbucks is feverishly working to bridge their business model from phase two to phase three. They are pushing to engage and support local communities and emphasize local sourcing in their marketing.

THE CHALLENGE OF THE NEW MODEL

Companies that are challenged the most by this new model are the ones that are still in phase one. They are the McDonald's and Walmarts of the new, global marketplace. Our traditional auto companies are also stuck in phase one. The old model of auto dealerships is being challenged by direct-to-buyer sales by innovators such as Tesla.

Innovative companies such as Uber, Google, Apple, and Tesla are busy building prototypes of electric and self-driving cars that will disrupt the whole auto industry. Phase three companies like these are seeking to meet personal consumer needs. Consumers no longer want to spend time behind the wheel of a car or contribute to global warming by burning fossil fuels.

In the beer sector, Coors and Budweiser are losing ground to smaller batch brewers such as Sierra Nevada and Craft Brew Alliance. Establishments such as Gordon Biersch have restaurants with breweries right on the premises. In Japan, restaurants and drinking establishments have sake houses right on-site.

In phase three, companies emphasize both the personal and local artisanship in their products and services. In phase three, all motion is localmotion. So if you have a business that's still in phase one, it's time to wake up. You'll need to adapt in a hurry and move quickly toward change.

THE LOCAL TOUCH

Every industry from food to fashion is being touched by

localmotion. As the shift continues, the individual will be even more paramount in company decision making.

Consider Domino's. The pizza chain has been something of a dormant brand, hardly part of the local movement. Yet they have to compete with local pizzerias. So they've begun to change their game with an Android app for customers to "build" and order their own pizzas, create their personal "pizza profile," and track their order.

Next up for Domino's is a reminder text based on a customer's order history, such as, "Hey, Jason, it's Friday. Would you like to preorder your large double cheese with mushrooms for dinner tonight?" For Domino's, it's a huge leap right into the kind of retail personalization that characterizes phase three of localmotion. Of course, the pizza chain still has a long way to go to phase three. How about locally sourced cheese?

As a health food chain, Whole Foods learned early on to embrace locally sourced products. Whole Foods is the ultimate phase two company. They tapped a niche market and helped bring what is healthy and important back to the food industry. In phase two, they call customer attention to their hormone-free dairy and meat products; their organic fruits, vegetables, and grains; and their specialty goat cheese made by a dairy farmer in the Netherlands.

Whole Foods is presently straddling the fence. They are in localmotion from phase two to phase three. They're in a big push to increasingly shift their identity to more local and regional products. To bring it home, they'll be introducing in-store kiosks where local vendors will sell goods and services. At Whole Foods, you'll meet local farmers selling greenhouse tomatoes, winter greens, and field corn. You'll find mini spas and tattoo kiosks, a local mom who makes artisanal soap in her kitchen. Whole Foods will not only be a destination for groceries but also a place for interacting with local artisans.

The local movement in food is exemplified by the popularity of farmers markets. Consumers increasingly want to be closer to their food and the people who grow it. They want to rub elbows with the farmer who sowed and harvested their zucchini. They want to talk with the baker who's selling that amazing banana bread with walnuts and raisins.

By endeavoring to become a local hub, Whole Foods illustrates localmotion in products, services, and experiences that embrace both the individual and the community. In doing so, it becomes more like a farmers market.

Major chains have begun to notice the trend and they're trying to make up lost ground. With more than 2,600 supermarket/department stores, Kroger is the fifth largest retailer in the world. Recently, it's come to recognize the local movement. It has introduced organic meats, milk, and produce. Its milk is "traceable," with the farmer's picture and location right on the carton. As a phase one company with a mass market model, Kroger is in localmotion toward phase two. It's getting on the local bandwagon to meet customer needs and individual desire for a healthy lifestyle.

WHAT DOES LOCAL REALLY MEAN?

Local isn't confined to just a city or town or even a fifty-mile radius that includes surrounding suburbs. The traditional neighborhood farmers market staffed by local vendors and farmers is just part of a much larger local picture. In the broadest sense, "locally sourced" products include coffee grown by hilltop farmers in Ecuador and handcrafted pottery made in New Mexico. It includes ecommerce platforms that connect local sellers to buyers globally.

The local, economic landscape puts the individual front and center. That individual can be either the buyer or the seller. Local commerce respects individual needs and wants and doesn't exploit labor. It's a movement away from mass production to artisanship. It's a trend away from factory farming to free-range meat and poultry.

Localmotion isn't exclusively about food. It's not simply

back to the land. The local movement embraces technology as the great equalizer. The wood-carver in Borneo can access a world market on the internet. Ecommerce companies such as Shopify and platforms such as eBay help individuals set up online stores, extending the global reach of artisans who live and work in remote locations.

Local includes computer applications, those many small, self-contained programs that are changing our world. When you think about it, apps are really designed for, and cater to, the individual.

For example, I travel quite a lot, so I've got a travel app that helps me understand and navigate the public transportation system in whatever city I'm visiting. I have another application that does currency conversion in real time. I use another app as a guide to local food and restaurants. Apps demonstrate how technology is a driver in our shift toward local.

It took creative innovation centered on the individual to bring apps to prominence. Applications are what made the Apple iPhone so much more powerful than other devices.

As a company, Apple's insight was to identify the phone as a device that can be tailored to the individual. Apple localized the iPhone. Mobile phones enable individual expression. A navigation application on my smartphone gets me from point A to point B by the fastest route. It tells me it'll take twenty-two minutes by car, or offers me alternative routes I can use with public transportation. It's my choice.

FROM EBAY TO ETSY AND BACK AGAIN

There's nothing new about handmade goods. Artisanship has been the way of the world for millennia. It's only relatively recently in the course of history that society shifted from local, individualized crafts to an industrialized, factory system of production and distribution.

But now, IT has turned the old paradigm on its head. Mass production has reached its limits because individuals want something different. At the same time, technology has caught up to individual needs, tastes, and desires.

For example, I, as an individual, appreciate well-crafted glassware. I heard about a Swedish brand called Kosta Boda that creates limited-edition glass sculptures. Each is designed by an individual artist and produced in small quantities. Although they are made in Sweden, I can purchase Kosta Boda collectables online and have them shipped directly to my home in Canada. I can learn about each artist, the techniques they use, and where they studied. The buying experience connects me to the product and to the artist who created it.

Global marketplaces such as China-based Alibaba are online marketing venues for millions of sellers. Alibaba, and its two other sites, Tmall and Taobao, is the largest ecommerce platform in the world, serving hundreds of millions of buyers. What is so fantastic about Alibaba is it helps local individuals peddle their wares worldwide. A beekeeper in Hunan Province can sell her honey directly to a buyer in Mexico City. A maple syrup producer in Vermont can sell his small-batch, grade A syrup to restaurants in Jinshi. Not only does the Chinese restaurateur get the syrup, but he also gets a story to go with the desserts he makes with it.

Another ecommerce platform, Shopify, enables small and medium-sized businesses to build their own online stores. Shopify extends the individual seller's reach to a global community interested in their products. The company was founded in 2004, launched in 2006, but didn't fully integrate its online stores and apps until 2009. It took another year for Shopify to launch mobile apps so that its merchants had mobile access. Sometimes it's technology that's playing catch-up to ideas. By 2015, Shopify went public and started trading at $28 a share.

Etsy is a peer-to-peer (P2P) ecommerce website that has taken local craft and individual artisans into a new era of online sales. It's something of an Amazon for handmade artisanal products. Etsy provides a platform for hard-to-find items from jewelry to paintings to vintage crafts. The company was launched in 2005, and by 2008 it was giving the old stalwart eBay a run for its money. To connect buyers and sellers in more personal ways, Etsy launched People Search, its own social networking system. When the company went public in 2015, its stock rose to $30 on the first day of trading.

The internet isn't new, and neither is artisanship. But the convergence of technology, social media, and evolving individual interests has been seeding new ways of exchanging goods. In this ever-widening context, "local" is a principle that is guiding new buying habits.

There are several hundred eBay millionaires in England. Each was a local dreamer who created their own shop in the eBay marketplace to sell kids clothing, eyeglasses, marbles, or whatever. That's how individualized eBay can be. And eBay was something of a pioneer in bringing together communities of people with like-minded buying and selling interests, a subject we'll explore more deeply in part two of this book.

UP CLOSE AND PERSONAL

In their own way, mass market companies such as Gillette have been trying to personalize the shaving experience for years. Their ad campaigns and razor designs have tried to frame shaving as a macho and sexy experience for men and as intimate and sexy for women. But there's nothing sexy about the price of razor blades, until now.

Upstart, online purveyors of shavers such as Dollar Shaving Club and Harry's have changed the mass market model. They've individualized shaving by selling blades cheaper by subscription. As a club member, you decide how often blades are sent to you based on your personal shaving needs. You're not paying for mass market ads and sponsorships; you're just paying for replacement blades, delivered to your door on a schedule you choose. Dollar Shaving Club brings shaving closer to home with personalized orders, but is there an even closer, more personal shave?

An even more up-close shave takes us back to our roots in the old-time barber shop. It's where "local" started in Main Street storefronts with barber poles spinning outside. You go in, shoot the breeze, catch up on sports scores and local gossip, and get the closest shave of your life. A hot towel to soften your stubble, a straight-edge razor honed on a leather strap, warm shaving foam, and a true, razor-sharp shave.

Ted Baker Grooming is a British fashion brand that's contemporary, slightly upscale, and at the forefront of personalization. Ted Baker's men's grooming shops exude a very cool atmosphere with highly trained, edgy barbers. The company's marketing concept is taken from the Turkish tradition of heated towels and close shaves, further adapted to individual needs and hair types. It's a consultative approach to grooming based on the premise that not all shaves are the same. People's beards are different and hair grows in different patterns with different textures. Ted Baker's salons reach for and deliver on an authentic and personal experience.

This push toward up close and personal is extending across many market sectors.

For decades, broadcast television and national brand advertisers ruled the TV world. Cable and satellite came along and introduced new options, hundreds of channels, and local access. But change was only beginning. An entirely new model of viewing was made possible by the juxtaposition of Wi-Fi enablement, fiber, better broadband, and streaming video.

New and more personalized digital viewing experiences became available through Netflix, Hulu, Amazon, YouTube, iTunes, and many more platforms worldwide. Now individuals can pick and choose and "curate" the movies and shows they want to see and when they want to see them. Mobile devices make it possible to do so wherever. Subscribers receive email alerts of new show releases based on their viewing preferences. Personalized entertainment is the new paradigm. You can hold it all in the palm of your hand on your mobile.

Car insurance is another case in point. Insurance has been an old-line industry for a long time now. Along the way, automobile insurers developed algorithms showing that women are safer drivers and that men aged eighteen to twenty-four are the most risky, so they pay more. When you think about it, however, a safe driver who happens to be twenty-three and male shouldn't be penalized by his demographic group. He shouldn't be paying the same rate as a risky driver with a poor driving record. But that's how the business is structured.

Yet we're starting to see change. Insurance companies are moving closer to tailoring rates to the individual based on how we drive. A strategic microchip placed in a vehicle can record and transmit speed, driving habits, distance covered, and time of day. It's already happening. Boomerang Insurance in Ontario advertises, "Drive safely and savings come back." They base your insurance premiums on your own personal driving record. Boomerang uses telematics—the technology behind GPS and navigation systems—to measure driving habits and reward safe drivers with discounts. They call it "usage-based insurance" (UBI) and reward their drivers without delay. Discounts show up on a customer's very next bill.

At its heart, Google is a company that has been focused on the individual. The Google search engine is designed to find what *you* are looking for. Search engines by their very nature are all about personalizing the search experience. What you type in the search field is what counts. The search is localized for you. It allows you to get to the end result of what you're looking for much faster. As a search tool, Google has striven to make online searches as relevant to the individual as possible.

One reason Google is such a successful company is it understood from the beginning that the individual matters. It's part of the company's philosophy. Google applied that same philosophy to its Android open-source, operating system. It designed Android for a whole slew of applications that allow the individual to personally tailor their Android device, whether they're in Japan, Nigeria, or Brazil.

And here's the key: By putting the individual first, Google reaches the masses. It's the polar opposite of old-school companies that design mass products and flood the market with advertising in hopes of reaching individual buyers.

THE INTERNET OF THINGS

As mentioned earlier, if we were to isolate a time when localmotion reached a tipping point, the year would be

2013. It was the point in time when individuals became empowered like never before.

Many things happened in 2013 to personalize the marketplace. For one thing, the company Nest came out with a unique home thermostat that hit the shelves extremely well. At the same time, 3-D printing, which had been around for several years, suddenly became affordable. Uber had also started earlier, but in 2013 the transportation company went mainstream across many cities and the Uber concept became sustainable. The year 2013 was also a magic number for Airbnb, when its P2P lodging started hitting critical mass.

It was as if the individual had finally hit the switch to become the localized center of commerce. Individuals had become the epicenter of how companies would distinguish themselves in a new, connected era.

The Nest Learning Thermostat was first introduced by Nest Labs in 2011 and was followed by Nest Protect smoke and carbon monoxide detectors in 2013. Nest products exemplify the internet of things.

The IoT is defined by a network of objects with embedded software that enables connectivity and the collection and exchange of data. Objects can be sensed and controlled remotely across a connected network.

The Nest Learning Thermostat did just that. What distinguished it was its machine-learning algorithm that could regulate home temperature according to customer preferences and location. It was programmable and Wi-Fi enabled, and could adjust automatically to learned data. The thermostat could be connected to the internet for updates and performance improvements. The device learned by the experience of a person's input. The company had harnessed technology to provide home temperature control that was centered on an individual's unique preferences and needs.

The IoT is bridging the gap between a person and their environment, between the things and services people use. Smart grids and smart homes, environmental monitoring, and big data are all part of the new IoT. It also includes intelligent shopping systems that track customers by their smartphones and refrigerator monitors that can inform a user's shopping list.

Imagine walking into a J. Crew store and the cashier knows you're on your way before you get there. You have a loyalty card loaded on your smartphone with a low-frequency Bluetooth sending a signal to the store saying, "Alex is coming." It would prompt the clerk to greet you when you arrive: "Hey, Alex. Good to see you. I see that last time you were at J. Crew you bought blue pants. Guess what? We've got this great khaki blazer if you're interested, and it's $10 off today."

The IoT is focused on the individual in local space: how people engage with their environment and how behavior changes the way things are done. As low-frequency Bluetooth becomes more cheaply available and embedded, we'll experience the interconnectedness of things even more.

Your Starbucks cashier will know who you are when you enter the store, as well as your typical order. You'll be walking past Dick's Sporting Goods and a promotion for Under Armour will ping your phone with a text. Nest products will connect to your car. As you near your home, your Nest device will know how close you are, and your home's climate will adjust automatically. Over time, your living space will be attuned to Wi-Fi live and respond to your distinct personal preferences in music, video entertainment, or a preheated oven. You'll be the epicenter of your home ecosystem.

SPEED, INTENSITY, AND DEPTH OF INTERACTION

What local means to the individual in today's world is the ability to interact with their surroundings, products, and services faster than ever before. Technology is the enabler of both the interaction and its speed. It also determines the intensity and depth of the interaction.

Speed determines how quickly an individual can get

information about a product or service, including qualities, specs, and cost. You can go to Best Buy and look at a computer you might buy, but with a smartphone in hand you can do a price comparison and get consumer reviews in that very moment in time. In your hand resides the speed, intensity, and depth of interaction to enhance your buying experience.

This is the new paradigm of localmotion—meeting and fully engaging an individual with a product or service in the moment. It means bringing the most sophisticated resources into play to meet the individual's pressing need in real time.

Companies need to be "individual smart" in the coming years. They will need to understand consumers at the individual level, not just as broad segments. The uniqueness of individuals and their changing tastes need to be learned and analyzed. AI will be able to identify the multiple variables that make up an individual; then it will allow corporations to be smart on how they approach individuals and speak to them.

HOW TO PERSONALIZE YOUR MARKETPLACE

Localmotion is moving businesses toward deeper personalization of goods and services. In this new consumer model, company decision making, product development, and marketing are shifting emphasis to local and regional needs and tastes. To better meet personal needs, retailers are increasingly seeking to position their stores as local hubs catering to individual preferences.

Technology is the main driver of innovation in the service of individual needs. This extends to the exchange of goods on ecommerce platforms, to the collection of data on personal tastes and buying habits, and to the personalization of software. A greater number of computer applications are now designed to solve the immediate needs of individuals to navigate life's complexities, from travel to mobile banking to ordering takeout.

Local is a core principle in social media where individual opinions have more influence over greater distances than ever before. Even as we curate our entertainment preferences using online platforms, we are offering our personal reviews and ratings to an ever-widening community of individuals.

This trend toward personalization has coalesced in the IoT, which enables individuals to engage with their environments through increased connectivity. IoT allows for advanced shopping systems that put an individual's immediate needs at the center of their own interconnected systems. This immediacy is advancing the speed and depth of interaction between individuals and the broader marketplace.

Search engines epitomize this emphasis on personal preferences. Online searches are designed to respond to the localized individual seeking information. Businesses are taking notice and making the shift from mass advertising to the personal approach to product development and marketing. From the devices we use to the clothing we wear, companies are seeking to tailor their products to individual needs and desires.

Chapter 2

WHY ARE YOU DRAWN TO LOCAL?

The shift toward local is in part a reaction to the dull sameness of shopping in urban centers across the globe. Our Main Streets and High Streets from New York to Singapore have been inundated with cookie-cutter chain stores selling similar goods. Local businesses have been pushed out by the likes of Starbucks, The Gap, and Banana Republic. Malls are no better, and people are pushing back. They aren't hungry for more Cheesecake Factorys but for uniqueness and innovation in the vast sea of sameness that has swallowed our cities and towns.

Traditional department stores, such as Nordstrom and Macy's, are basically middlemen fed by the same supply chain. New fashions are introduced during spring and fall fashion weeks, and a few months later they show up on racks at our major retailers. Some traditional retailers interested in controlling more of their margin have even developed their own brand labels.

In a new paradigm shift, however, the iconic British fashion house Burberry began selling directly online, cutting out the middleman. It was a bid not only for increased sales but also as a way to get closer to its customers. By taking down the barrier between the end user and the manufacturer, Burberry altered the relationship between designer and wearer. It changed the equation for how a luxury fashion house that was founded in 1856 does business in today's changing marketplace.

CONTEXTUAL BUYING

Knowing the individual, their wants, desires, and propensities is at the core of online and social media marketing today. Smart companies want to know about a person's habits and transactions. Basically, they want to know what you want to buy. And when they think they know, they want to put it right in front of you. This is called contextual buying or advertising.

You see it all the time when surfing the web. If you spend time on a sports website, you're not surprised to see ads targeting you for new running shoes. Google AdSense uses contextual advertising and sells the service to millions of online merchants.

Those shoes you viewed on Zappos, that barbecue grill you saw on Amazon, that movie you almost watched on Netflix can start showing up in ads on your browser.

Uber understands contextual buying. It isn't so much a cab company as a transportation company that wants to be there when you need it. It's an app on your mobile device that you can access at any moment. It's 6:15 p.m. on a Friday, it's raining, and you need a ride from work to a bar downtown. It's 2:00 a.m. on a Saturday night, it's last call, and you definitely need a ride home. You don't even have to reach into your wallet; payment is taken care of in the Uber app.

PayPal knows you buy on the fly, so it's got a company called Braintree that enables ecommerce and one-touch mobile payments from anywhere. Mobile payment companies such as LevelUp and CARDFREE are all about customer loyalty and brand building with personalized offers, targeted rewards, and customer engagement in real time.

As a mobile payment platform, LevelUp offers expedited payments from consumers directly to local businesses. It meets the in-moment needs of both the buyer and the merchant. LevelUp and CARDFREE offer special rainmaker settings for merchants. By a deft use of data analytics, they can tailor deals and offers for consumers on behalf of their merchant clients.

It's a cold, snowy day in Buffalo, and you receive an online discount for hot clam chowder at a local eatery. That's contextual relevancy in the moment and right on time.

Odeon, the UK cinema chain, had a challenge drawing customers to its theaters when the weather was bad. One solution it came up with was to change ticket prices on the fly and offer discounts to specific theater locations based on demand. It's the same concept of an airline basing ticket price on availability. Airlines do this really well. Regular flyers know it's cheaper to book a flight for a Tuesday when fewer people fly.

Why can't theaters do the same thing? A cinema chain could say, "You know what? It's really bad weather and we'll be selling way below capacity. Why not incentivize people to come out? Give them $2 off or a complimentary popcorn and bring them in." In this way, theaters can manage their yields.

Small companies are driving this innovation. We've already mentioned Uber, and as you'll see, we'll mention them again. Unlike the pricing of traditional cab companies, Uber prices fluctuate based on demand. It's called "surge pricing," and in Uber's case, prices rise when the weather is bad, or there's a ball game, or it's New Year's Eve and demand is extremely high. Drivers like it because they earn more, but customers definitely don't. They tend to feel put upon and gouged when they need a cab most. Uber is taking steps to remedy customer perception by better notifying riders of price fluctuations and calling rider attention to reduced wait and trip times.

Gift cards are another case in point. Gift card sales is a $150 billion industry, but until recently, it has been anonymous. If the card is purchased with cash, a business will have no clue who the user is. The person who buys the card is anonymous and the person they give it to is also anonymous. From the business perspective, there's no real touch point with the customer, which is materially difficult and challenging. However, if a person buys an iTunes or Starbucks gift card using their credit card, the company knows who bought it, it knows where the card was bought, and at what time of day. It's developing a picture of the card, its buyer, and potential user because gift cards capture customer data.

Supermarkets and chain stores build customer loyalty with in-store discount cards. Those cards also mine data about sales and generate discount coupons at checkout. Businesses are highly motivated to know the buying habits of their customers and to shape their shopping experience.

Smart retailers are now selling their gift cards in-house, rather than depending on sales from gift card racks at retail chains. They want to cut out the middleman, not just to avoid paying a percentage but also to get more up close and personal with their customers. Starbucks sells its cards directly and applies them to its loyalty program. It wants to connect its customer to the brand. It wants to track that card and get to know its customers by their buying habits, their drink orders, and their likes and tastes. By better understanding the individual, the company can deepen and personalize the Starbucks experience.

At SambaConnects, we want to tailor gift experiences to individual tastes. It's similar to a friend wanting to buy a gift they know will be appreciated. We facilitate gift giving by following the path of the gift experiences we sell. If it's for a winery, which winery, in which region? How many people purchased that wine tour through us? When a person or couple book their tour, it's an opportunity to connect with them and provide incentives for more gift giving and receiving.

Personalized promotions and customer-specific offers are enabled by big data. It's highly localized selling built around interacting with the customer. It's contextual buying based on individual habits. The function of business is to understand the customer, what they buy, how often, and how much they spend. It doesn't come on a spreadsheet. You get it on a database that provides the kind of information that will help a company communicate with customers as close to real time as possible.

This is why gift cards are gradually shifting to mobile applications allowing individuals to buy digitally and gift digitally via smartphones. Digital purchasing provides traceable links to who the purchaser is, who the gift recipient is, and how they use the digital "card." Companies can begin to create a map of the individual using the digital gift, including how often they use it, when, and how much they spend.

In this new paradigm, customers are attracted to the businesses that serve them best and know them best. A phase one company such as Walmart that's structured entirely around price and value will miss out on the opportunity to connect with customers directly and personally. By not leveraging the new localized marketplace, it'll be left behind.

EMOTIONAL CONNECTION

In 2008, BlackBerry was at the height of its popularity as a mobile device. However, in short order, BlackBerry's success was usurped by Apple. All Apple did was introduce the iPhone with all its technical ease and customizable applications. Apple took all of the emotional equity it had built with customers over the years and basically communicated, "Guess what? Here's Apple's version of a mobile phone made just the way you want it. You can use it for whatever's important to you."

Brands with better emotional connection have a better chance of succeeding with consumers. Lululemon is one of them. The yoga-wear company, which started in Vancouver, is built on a concept of health and wellness in the context of both the individual and community. Chip Wilson, who started the company, promoted his yoga-wear products by offering them free to yoga instructors. In exchange, the instructors became "ambassadors" for Lululemon, introducing Wilson's yoga products to their classes. Lululemon stores were opened throughout Canada, the United States, the United Kingdom, as well as Japan and China. In fact, Wilson chose the name Lululemon to concentrate Asian attention on a brand name they found difficult to pronounce.

Sold only through Lululemon, the yoga apparel was tailored for an emotional connection to health and well-being, peace of mind, and self-awareness. The design of the stores, the demeanor of the sales clerks, the in-store yoga classes all catered to a yoga consciousness.

Lululemon was launched as the yoga craze took off. Then, at the height of its success, the brand faltered due to a fabric glitch. In 2013, devotees of the apparel began to notice that Lululemon's custom fabric, called Luon, had become too sheer and therefore too revealing. The company dealt with the challenge by issuing a recall and promising to make it up to its customers. Meanwhile, lovers of the brand sought vintage apparel on the Lululemon Exchange on Facebook until the company's new clothing line made it out to the stores. Like Apple, which had suffered a setback when product lines diverged from the company's founding standard, Lululemon retained its loyal fan base by a return to its original quality standard.

CUSTOMER PSYCHE

Uber is a phase three success story precisely because its founders understood the psyche of their customers. The Uber concept was developed by two friends who wanted the ease of tapping into an app to get a ride while visiting other countries. Uber was able to launch precisely because the technology of mobile phone penetration was there to support it. Uber jumped into the market to fill a consumer need for fast, reliable transportation that could be accessed from anywhere at any time. Local individuals and groups were enabled to book a ride from a mobile device and be picked up by a local driver.

Uber shook up the transportation industry and took a slice of the market. Consumers can download the Uber app and view a map to see where drivers are in their vicinity. In this way, Uber revolutionized the local transportation landscape. In order to compete, many local taxi companies had to up their game by digitizing access to their cabs.

The founders knew their customers' need because they knew their own personal need for dependable, local transportation when out and about. By tapping the customer's transportation need in a new localized way, Uber tapped into the customer's psyche—the way the customer thinks and feels. It also tapped into a trend of our times—what the Germans call *zeitgeist*—in which urban millennials are less inclined to own their own vehicles and more inclined to rent and share. It's an attitudinal shift.

This new economic model of a sharing economy is the same millennial zeitgeist behind Airbnb. The company's founders were roommates who were having a hard time coming up with rent money in San Francisco. They hit on the idea of getting inflatable airbeds and renting them out as lodging in their loft, and Airbnb was born. It's an updated version of the traditional bed and breakfast with accessibility through a website and mobile applications. Airbnb brings guests and hosts together and facilitates online payments.

The financial crisis of 2008 dashed consumer faith in banks. Overleveraged financial institutions had been preying on consumers and investing in bad mortgages. Loss of trust in the old order wound up fueling a local movement in lending and investing. People found out that they really didn't like the anonymity of not knowing how their money was being channeled through the banking system. Public skepticism was driven in part by the same factors that birthed the local food movement. In the same way that consumers want to know where and how their food is grown, they want to know where and how their retirement savings are being invested.

As a reaction, money management entered the local movement. Alternative banking embraced new financial technologies that allow for more localized and personalized saving and investing. "Microlending" of small amounts at low interest has helped startups and small businesses raise money. Microlenders are more development oriented than profit driven. They want to help small entrepreneurs get started on the path to financial self-sufficiency. "P2P lending" is a similar system of connecting small lenders to borrowers who pay lower interest rates than they would at banks.

Another development in the local financial movement and startup community is "crowdfunding." It's an internet-based, alternative model of raising capital for business through many supporters who aren't the typical venture capitalist. Instead of a few people holding large amounts of equity in a company, many people hold much smaller pieces and pool their funding. Hundreds of crowdfunding platforms are available through online portals from FundAnything to RocketHub.

Crowdfunding is an outgrowth of "crowdsourcing," which helps people create businesses at the local level. In crowdsourcing, business advisors gather online to share their expertise with startups to develop product and business plans.

Kickstarter is a crowdfunding platform based around the arts and creative expression. To date, Kickstarter has raised almost $2 billion in online pledges from close to ten million backers. They've helped finance music, film, and video games, among more than 250,000 creative projects. They represent a global community of investors who want to bring ideas to life. Banks are not part of the transaction at all.

When the traditional functions of banks and financial services from saving and investing to lending and funding enter the local movement, it's clear that major change is happening across the institutional marketplace.

CONSUMER PACKAGED GOODS

Savvy customers in the second decade of the twenty-first century want products that are personalized to their specific needs. More importantly, they want to be able to interact with brands, especially brands they already know and like.

For instance, if I were a diaper manufacturer such as Pampers, I'd want to increase my brand's connection to young parents. And if I were a young parent, I'd want Pampers to ship diapers to my home on a prearranged schedule. Both sides of the relationship—buyer and seller—basically have the same goal in mind.

When Apple launched its own retail stores, many people thought it was crazy. Why go to all the expense when you can easily sell online or through existing retail chains? Apple knew better. It was certain that no one else could convey its brand better than it could. It knew its customers better than anyone else did. So it engaged industrial designer Marc Newson to design its stores, and the stores reflect Apple's style right down to the screws and fasteners used in displays. For an Apple customer who wants a product that meets their individual tech and design needs, an Apple store is the only place to go.

Godiva markets its chocolates in multiple venues, from Macy's to Walgreens, but if you want personalized chocolate gifts and baskets, Godiva has you covered. Godiva Chocolatier boutiques prepare signature truffles and confections, wedding favors, and personalized gifts for all occasions. In this way, the company curates its product to meet individual needs in direct, one-on-one retail in an atmosphere of virtual chocolate heaven that drives home the brand.

THE DRAW OF LOCAL

Across the wide spectrum of business and industry, smart companies are jumping on the localmotion train, finding innovative ways to create and engage customer loyalty. Barriers between seller and buyer are coming down, and relationships in the marketplace are changing rapidly.

At the heart of this change is personalization. It occurs when the individual is interacting with a brand, a product, or a system, such as Amazon picking up on browsing history and offering buying suggestions. Sophisticated algorithms monitor taste, lifestyle, and patterns of behavior, delivering content that's relevant to the individual.

Driving these changes are innovation in IT and AI coupled with social, economic, and generational forces. By our very nature, individuals are drawn to convenience and connection. From the moment we are born, we crave responsiveness in our relationships.

In the marketplace, from transportation to banking, clothing to confections, we increasingly want our personal and communal needs met. We want to do business with companies who care as much about individuals and communities as we do.

HOW TO MAKE RETAIL UP CLOSE AND PERSONAL

Savvy retailers who want to get closer to individual customers
are eliminating the middlemen. By tracking the personal buying
habits of customers, they are learning what individuals want
and when they want it. This is called contextual buying and it
is taking down barriers between end users and manufacturers.

Small companies are driving this innovation with personalized
promotions and customer-specific offers based on data gathering. They are getting to know their customers in a localized
method of selling and buying. By engaging IT and AI, companies can gather browsing history and monitor individual
tastes and buying patterns to deliver products and services
that are most relevant to consumers.

In this new retail model, businesses are striving to get more up
close and personal with their customers in real time. They are
mining sales data to better understand customer tastes and
build deeper emotional connections. What began with the local
food movement now extends to the broader marketplace, from
consumer packaged goods to banking and money management.

This draw toward a personalized marketplace represents a
shift of mindset in customers who increasingly want to interact with their favorite brands. Customers don't want to be
anonymous. They want connection and they want to spend
their dollars with companies that share their values.

Chapter 3

HOW MUCH DOES THE LOCAL MOVEMENT TOUCH YOUR LIFE?

Prior to starting Samba Days, I was head of consumer marketing for Aeroplan, one of Canada's largest customer loyalty programs. It started off twenty-five years ago as a frequent flyer points program for Air Canada, then expanded to include credit card spending. What it taught me is that personalization and connection to customers is paramount.

A business rises or falls on its ability to understand customer needs and behavior. In our digital age with so much competition online and in multiple retail venues, companies need to reach out and touch customers' lives.

CLOSE AS SKIN

When we consider how much the shift toward local touches the lives of individuals, I'm reminded of personalization in a completely different industry—cosmetics.

In the ever-expanding marketplace, one of the best loyalty programs I've seen is Beauty Insider. It's associated with Sephora, a one-stop shop for beauty products with more than 1,700 locations in thirty countries. Sephora sells many different brands, and it has lots of competition. It competes not only with department stores and pharmacy chains but also with the brands it represents.

What Sephora has done to set itself apart, however, is to design its loyalty program entirely around personalization. The Beauty Insider program draws customers by tailoring products according to each customer's unique characteristics. An innovative Color IQ app defines a person's skin tone and their contextual needs, such as lifestyle, work, time of day, event, and clothing. Sephora has determined that there are at least 110 different skin tone variations, as well as facial characteristics, that determine makeup selections and combinations to match the individual.

Customers register and provide the necessary details, and Beauty Insider crunches the data to make product recommendations. In the traditional world of over-the-counter makeup, a customer relies on the subjective opinion of cosmetics counter staff to make the best color match. It's usually a trial-and-error process.

Sephora's Beauty Insider program takes the guesswork out of cosmetics selection by empowering the individual to make choices based on a huge field of data. It's an enormous differentiator, and it allows customers to choose from among many brands in different price ranges. With Beauty Insider, Sephora has done an amazing job of leveraging customer loyalty.

INDIVIDUAL TASTE

Coca-Cola has shifted its marketing gears many times through the years, so it's revealing to follow its recent promotional choices. The Share a Coke campaign, which began in spring 2013, is centered on self-expression, relationships, and emotional connection.

With Share a Coke, the company took an innovative step by introducing personalized Coke bottles. It was a completely new concept. Coca-Cola gave consumers the ability to express themselves and share the experience with friends and family by gifting bottles emblazoned with personal names. The campaign garnered more than 500,000 photos on Twitter with the hashtag #shareacoke, and gained some twenty-five million Facebook followers.

With this campaign, Coke put the individual customer front and center, and people responded. For its pilot launch, Coke crunched the data on names in Australia and filled grocery coolers with bottles covering the nation's top 150 names. The campaign eventually ran in seventy countries and has sold more than 150 million personalized bottles. The result has been a 2 percent increase in Coke sales, a major increase in the soft drink industry.

A buyer can place an online order to personalize a bottle for $5. Almost anything goes. A customer in the UK proposed to his girlfriend with four bottles, each emblazoned with one of four words: "Will You Marry Me?" He took a picture of the bottles waiting for her in the refrigerator, posted it on social media, and the photo went viral. It's a remarkable example of how the local movement in marketing can touch people's lives.

Another brand took a similar tack by partnering with a renowned UK department store. The most popular spread worldwide, next to jam, is Nutella. In the last few years, the chocolate hazelnut spread has become something of a hip addition to foods. There are doughnuts filled with Nutella, cakes, icings, you name it. People can't get enough of the stuff, so Nutella teamed with Selfridges & Co., the century-old, high-end department store chain to make its product even more appealing.

They parked a cute little Nutella truck in front of Selfridges in London and people queued up to order their personalized bottles of the spread. Their timing was perfect, right before Christmas, but it was a one-off event. Nutella never scaled the success of the event in the way Coca-Cola scaled Share a Coke.

When Sweden's Absolut ventured into the vodka market, it made a splash by personalizing every bottle it distributed—not with individual names but rather with artwork. For a short time, it engaged artists to paint every bottle by hand. Each bottle became a unique showpiece that would appeal to individual tastes. The campaign was so successful that mainstream artists joined in designing bottles that then became collectible.

GETTING TO KNOW YOU

These days, customers typically search products online before buying in a store. They want to compare competitive products, prices, and buying options before shopping. Retailers therefore have to be nimble and engaged online in order to attract customers to their brick-and-mortar stores. Smart retailers have begun merging the online experience with the local retail world. They are personalizing the retail experience by tying digital and physical worlds together.

In the world of fashion retail, few do it better than Nordstrom. The retailer's marketing team curates its in-store offerings based on customer interest online. They create Pinterest pages on trending products and disseminate pages through social media. Then, depending on what customers pick and identify as their preferences, Nordstrom will match stock in their stores. It's almost like virtual focus groups, learning from customers the products they'd like to buy locally.

When customers arrive at the store, Nordstrom takes it to the next level. It uses Wi-Fi sensors to track customer smartphones, gathering data on where in the store customers are browsing. It uses this information to feed the customer's on-site journey. It collects data on foot traffic, the number of people who are in the store at a given time, and which customers have the Nordstrom app. It's a sophisticated funnel of activity that allows the retailer to understand customer behavior.

It's also an opportunity for the retailer to make suggestions. If a customer is browsing dress shoes, they might receive a ping on their phone alerting them to a sale on ALDO men's oxfords. If you visit the store often, Nordstrom knows your distinct profile and tastes.

The retailer also collects and analyzes social data. Nordstrom has three million Facebook fans, 4.4 million Pinterest followers, and more than a half million followers on Twitter. It can link up a customer's preferences with available stock. What retailers want most is to put products out there that customers want to buy. Wi-Fi and social media allow them access to individual taste preferences like never before. That Hugo Boss suit, the blue one with a striped tie that you viewed on Nordstrom's Pinterest page, will follow you to Facebook, just in case you need another look.

Some companies have begun applying data gathering to determine employee behavior. For example, one publicly traded company uses an algorithm to spot which staff members are ready to quit versus who is investing in the company's employee stock options. The company correlates employees who dump company stock in chunks to those who are most likely to quit. Recognizing the pattern is the first step for the company to get in front of the situation. It's an opportunity to intervene and engage the employee before the fact in order to increase retention.

DIGITAL SMARTS

As mentioned earlier, artificial intelligence is shaping the culture of how individuals connect with products and services. At the root of AI is predictability of human behavior. It can be applied to computerized systems, video games, predictive shopping, fraud detection, music apps, you name it. Some 90 percent of people have smartphones.

These are more than simply communication devices. What makes a phone smart is software that enables access to the internet, downloading of applications, data calculation, among so many other capacities. Yet this level of smarts is just the tip of the iceberg.

A few years ago, tech giants Apple, Google, and Microsoft woke up to the concept of creating more proactive features that could help users solve everyday problems. It was the dawn of the digital assistants Siri, Google Now, and Cortana.

Now we can phrase questions and commands and get results at our fingertips: Where is the nearest Chinese restaurant? What's on my schedule today? Remind me to call Jerry at eight o'clock. What's the weather? Digital assistants help us navigate our environment by continuously learning about us, and as the intelligence of user data becomes richer, they can increasingly anticipate our needs.

For example, the tech startup DigitalGenius has successfully applied AI to automate customer service support. Its platform uses machine learning and natural language processing (NLP) to engage with customers and answer their questions. It crunches FAQs, the most frequently asked customer service questions, into a digital network. It also links email, transcripts, Facebook pages, Twitter feeds, and more as reference points to push the algorithms. This provided deeper, more customer-centric responses.

Another innovative AI personal assistant is "Amy (or Andrew) Ingram." Developed by a company called x.ai, Amy is an executive assistant that does highly sophisticated scheduling. The x.ai software is used by LinkedIn, Uber, Spotify, and other leading-edge companies. Of course, the application is also available to individuals. Amy understands natural language to the extent that it can process input from conversations and digital communications to automatically schedule meetings and calls. By sifting and linking data, Amy functions at a deeper level of personalization than Siri or Cortana.

Clara, the personal assistant developed by Clara Labs, manages meetings and scheduling by a simple handoff in an email. By cc'ing Clara, the user delegates the task and the exchange of emails that leads to the meeting date and time. Clara is used by organizations as diverse as Stripe, Houzz, and AngelList.

This is only the beginning. As AI, machine learning, and algorithms become more sophisticated, it won't be us telling Siri what to do but rather Siri informing us of what we should be doing.

AI is also extremely valuable in countering fraud and

theft online. Financial institutions and online sellers are under increasing pressure to combat cybercrime and the systematic fraud involved in stealing customers' personal information. In a recent case involving the cybertheft of a company's Amazon gift card codes, some $4 million in codes were hijacked.

To guard against cyberattacks, companies are arming themselves with digital tools such as Mastercard's Design Intelligence. It uses AI technology to provide institutions with accurate, real-time information about transactions. Design Intelligence is capable of learning buying patterns at the individual level based on transaction history. Mastercard as well as Visa and American Express are creating algorithms based on individual behavior rather than just generic purchasing patterns.

On the flip side, Amazon is creating a score card for fraud. It uses a machine learning tool for ecommerce that ascertains individual profiles on a scale of one hundred. The AI tool can weigh the profile scale based on the customer's past transactions. Suspicious transactions are analyzed and, if determined to be of sufficient risk, overridden, saving the individual and their financial institution considerable trouble.

PERSONALIZED RETAIL

Target calls its Cartwheel app "a whole new spin on coupons." It's a made-for-mobile application that gives shoppers access to digital coupons and discounts that can be scanned at checkout. The user selects from hundreds of offers that are added to a personalized barcode on their smartphone.

At the same time, Target uses the app to track and understand customer preferences. The company uses data analytics to understand customer choices and create personalized content. An extensive marketing team analyzes and crunches numbers to push relevant content promotions and offers to mobile applications. It's the basis of predictive shopping, understanding a customer's choices and habits in order to target appropriate promotions to the right customers. A customer is tracked in-store as well as online during browsing or making purchases on the Target website. For a retailer, it's the next best thing to having a crystal ball.

Upward of fifteen million people have downloaded the mobile app because they want the best shopping deals. During the holiday buying season from November to December, 60 percent of them are active shoppers using Cartwheel. Target knows what they've clicked on and which products interest them the most. Then it can serve up coupons to match customer preferences. It's win-win all around.

Retailers have a challenge in trying to push the boundaries of what's happening now into the future. An example of this is Topshop, a UK boutique clothing brand catering to teens to late twenties. Topshop has been implementing new "augmented reality" technologies into the shopping experience. Its stores have virtual fitting rooms where customers can select specific garments on a large digital screen to see how they would look wearing those items. It's like a magic mirror in which the customer can see how they'd look without physically trying on the clothing. It's like having a personal valet, or a "virtual valet," right there in the fitting room.

In another innovation, Topshop teamed with Facebook in 2012 to create an interactive show at London Fashion Week. They engaged potential buyers online and at the same time monitored their behavior and tastes to inform design decisions. More than two million people were digital participants in the Customize the Catwalk event.

The following year, Topshop partnered with Google+ at London's Tate Modern museum to livestream a unique Fashion Week show on YouTube and Google+. Specialized cameras provided virtual front-row seats to four million viewers far beyond the usual clique of fashion elites and journalists. As a streetwear brand, Topshop wanted to reach out directly to its customers and enable them to instantly buy products. In doing so, it eliminated the middlemen and the huge time lag between Fashion Week and getting product out to retailers.

In designer Rebecca Minkoff's showrooms and fitting rooms in New York, customers can interact with digital screens to view look books and select products, or to even order free beverages—coffee or champagne, anyone? Minkoff has taken digital components of online shopping to ground level and further personalized the in-person shopping experience.

This is the kind of personalization in buying that information technology is enabling. As an interesting aside, the first retailer to use a version of augmented reality fitting was the fashion house Burberry. Later, the CEO of Burberry became head of Apple's retail division. Why? Because retail and technology are meshing in the marketing space and Apple wanted to seize the moment.

PERSONALIZED SELECTION

Pandora, the music streaming app, has its own take on using AI to match music selections to the individual user. Unlike Spotify and other popular music streaming apps, Pandora's system doesn't rate music by genre, customer selection, or by correlation to other listeners' choices. Instead, the company uses a radical approach that analyzes a recording's musical structure against four hundred attributes, such as melody, harmony, rhythm, and lyrics, to define distinctive musical genomes.

The company consulted thirty AI experts who spent five years analyzing the works of ten thousand musical artists to create a vast catalog of recordings. By mapping recordings according to genome, Pandora personalizes selections to a greater degree than by listener behavior or reviews. It goes deeper than any musical category, such as blues, to the distinctive melodies, harmonies, rhythms, and other traits that define particular styles of blues compositions.

It's similar to how medicine is becoming more personalized through understanding human DNA as a factor in prescribing medication and treatment. Mapping the human genome translates in the world of music to mapping the musical genome.

YOUR 3-D WORLD

Your world is going to change dramatically over the next ten years. The Industrial Revolution and the assembly line will be giving way to 3-D printing. What's driving this change is the localization and personalization of products, along with advances in robotics. 3-D printing will eliminate the need for volume manufacturing necessary to justify expensive industrial machinery. Manufactured items will be individualized.

With 3-D printing, a single product or part can be custom-ized on an individual basis. It reduces and eliminates the need for making thousands at a time. With computer-aided design (CAD), a designer can finish a piece and send a signal to a 3-D printer that basically says, "Print this piece for me." The 3-D printer generates layer after layer after layer of a single finished piece. It could be a lug nut for a tractor or a pair of eyeglasses.

In fact, the German eyeglass company Mykita has already introduced 3-D-printed eyewear. The technology is uniquely suited to eyeglasses. Traditionally, to buy eye-glasses you walk into a shop and try on a dozen or more frames. Most of the time, you can't even see what you're doing because you need prescription glasses to see. You try on several pairs hoping to gain an impression in a mirror, and you wind up asking strangers' opinions.

At Mykita, eyewear is now customizable to the shape and width of a person's head, the bridge of their nose, the rise of their cheekbones, the shape of their eyes, all the unique features of an individual's face. A designer with a 3-D printer can create eyewear that is perfectly suited to individual contours, style preferences, and personal tastes. It's worlds apart from the way things are usually done.

As in the world of eyewear, so too in the world of toys. Hasbro is in the process of personalizing toy buying by partnering with 3D Systems, one of the first companies to commercialize 3-D printing. The toy company wants to make it possible for an individual to personalize their own My Little Pony online. The buyer could select pony color, hair color, and eye color, among other distinguishing characteristics, to personal choice.

The power of 3-D printing extends to edible products as well. 3D Systems has partnered with Hershey's to personalize chocolate confections. In a twist on the Hershey's Kiss, the company can offer numerous personalized versions printed with 3-D technology according to the many variations of personal taste. In another variation, 3D Systems partnered with the confectioner Sugar Lab to personalize party cake decorations, icing, labels, and themes.

At the Massachusetts Institute of Technology, advances in 3-D printing have seen the creation of robotic arms that can be used in building construction. Free-moving robots can weld or spray foam to create individualized structures and components of any size. Another 3-D robotic prototype at the Oak Ridge National Laboratory successfully printed a mobile home as well as a utility vehicle that can pull it.

In athletic footwear, New Balance is a time-honored, forward-thinking brand. Using technology developed by the Swedish startup Volumental, New Balance has introduced a global launch of 3-D foot scanners at five hundred of their stores. This sophisticated scanning yields personalized recommendations for the right footwear to match the exact contours of a customer's feet.

"We are building a world that fits you," is Volumental's slogan, and they mean it. Other global retailers, such as Lotte in Korea and the ski boot company BootDoc, have embraced the company's foot scanning as well. Behind the technology are advances in computer vision and machine learning, and as 3-D printing evolves, the next phase will be footwear printed and knitted automatically to match the individual.

In the long run, 3-D printing will reduce waste and shrink the environmental footprint. We won't have to manufacture billions of things. So many of our everyday items will be created on an individual, as-needed basis.

ERGONOMICS IS PERSONAL

Ergonomics looks at the applied science of equipment design in the workplace. In an example of applied ergonomics, Herman Miller, the office furniture manufacturer, has incorporated ergonomics research into how individuals work to produce personalized options in its designs. The company observed, surveyed, and analyzed individuals in office settings to ascertain personal needs in equipment use, from desks to chairs, to cabinets and other equipment.

In chair design, it looked beyond the limitations of height and swivel adjustment to create the Aeron Chair. With a mesh bottom and back, the Aeron Chair was designed for air circulation and individual comfort adjustment of armrests, lumbar support, seat depth, tilt, and tension, among other qualities. It's billed as "the seat that performs for you."

GETTING EXTREMELY PERSONAL

In the realm of predicting personal preferences and patterns of behavior based on millions of pieces of information, Facebook excels. Facebook is an important marketing platform for thousands of companies. Of all social media, Facebook is well positioned to know individual users intimately, based on their Facebook activity and the company they keep. In this way, the company can effectively commercialize individual preferences by providing offers based on what a person likes and clicks on. However, the platform can go even further by crunching data to actually predict the evolution and demise of romantic relationships.

Based on patterns of user activity, Facebook's data scientists have determined that if a relationship lasts more than three months on Facebook, there's a high probability it will survive for years. It turns out that three months is the first hurdle and probably the most material moment of a relationship. The company's researchers have determined that people share the standing of their romantic relationship on Facebook when they are serious about it.

By looking at connections in communications patterns, Facebook can even predict who might be in a relationship next. It's hard to believe, but IT can even predict our relationships before we do.

INTRUSION OR CONVENIENCE?

Using data to personalize experiences and drive customer loyalty will continue to grow and evolve. Whether it's DigitalGenius using applied AI to automate customer service support, or digital assistants such as Siri and Cortana helping individuals to organize their lives, machine learning is getting better at understanding user behavior.

Localized commerce tailored to the individual is the driving force behind Rebecca Minkoff's showrooms, Mykita's 3-D-printed eyewear, and the Aeron Chair. Personalized selection is at the root of Pandora's music streaming app and Apple's retail stores. Predictive understanding of behavior can guard against cyberattacks, as with Mastercard's Design Intelligence, or foresee a romantic break shaping up on the pages of Facebook.

To some, it's personal intrusion, but to others, it's a new dawn of convenience. Perhaps it's only a matter of degree or the manner in which new technologies are used or abused. We're still in the process of seeing how it will all shake out in the marketplace.

Connection to customers is the mainstay of personalization. In an age of online buying and multiple sales venues, a company's success depends on its ability to understand customers and touch lives. Loyalty programs that engage customers and offer opportunities for self-expression and shared experience are leading the way in marketing. Companies that put the individual first are learning to leverage customer loyalty.

These companies engage with customers online and merge the online experience with local retail. They are making the leap between digital and in-store sales. Sellers are gathering data on customer behavior both online and in stores to develop sophisticated funnels that steer buying. Sellers can profile distinct buying habits and analyze social media data to link customer preferences to available products.

AI is changing how individuals connect with products, services, and brands by adding predictability to the mix. Machine learning and natural language processing are engaging customers in ways that provide new reference points for customer service and product development and placement. Mobile smartphone applications are providing customers with personalized offers and discounts that can be scanned at checkout.

At the same time, 3-D printing is beginning to individualize the way products are manufactured. 3-D printing makes it possible to customize products on an individual basis, from eyewear to toys, to clothing and building materials. Personalized options are also becoming available in the applied science of equipment design. Ergonomics research has led to design changes in the workplace that cater to how individuals work. In this way, technology and retail work hand in hand to personalize buying.

The ability to track and understand customer choices through data analytics lays the groundwork for predictive shopping. Social media has been instrumental in commercializing individual preferences by crunching data to predict behavior. Marketing teams are becoming more sophisticated in targeting relevant promotions to the right customers based on both online and in-store browsing. As these factors continue to unfold, brands will increasingly connect with customers and touch lives in the marketplace.

THE COMMUNITY

Chapter 4

HOW BUSINESS BUILDS COMMUNITY

In part one, we focused on how the individual is becoming more empowered in the marketplace. The new economic landscape has been changed by local sourcing and personalization as companies are increasingly addressing individual needs in their products and services. Advances in IT have enabled new forms of local consumerism from Uber to Airbnb, to Shopify. In part two, we'll be looking at how this local movement is aggregating around communities.

In this new paradigm, businesses want to both help and influence what people gain collectively from a product or service. In the old paradigm, companies didn't listen much. They bombarded consumers with marketing campaigns and promotions until they finally realized that people weren't listening either.

Consumers have matured and aren't buying the old sell anymore. They've moved on. IT has increasingly enabled online commerce, rapid communication, and interaction through social media. Consumers are attracted to inspiring new companies and startups that understand their needs. We've seen how companies are listening and tailoring products and services to meet individual needs. Smart companies are also learning to think about groups of people who share like-minded opinions and tastes. After all, communities are built on like-minded individuals.

HOW TO BE SMART

Smart companies have learned to see the larger aggregate of individuals as communities. They understand their customers as people who share similar tastes, ideas, ways of seeing the world, and interacting with others. These companies are shaping their products and services, their outreach and communication around their customer communities.

Much of this new thinking is driven by the generation of millennials, who are highly group oriented and more communal than previous generations. We're at an important turning point when new products and services are reflecting a new collective culture. Millennials represent a collaborative culture, less based on the individual, more centered on the group. They are more outgoing and inclusive, less suspicious and enclosed. Social media is their enabler.

Millennials care less about owning and more about access. Their way of thinking is, "I don't need to own a house or a car. I can rideshare with Lyft, or car share a Zipcar." Renting suits them. They don't mind staying at a stranger's house with Airbnb when they travel; they don't need a hotel chain. All of these changes in attitude are upsetting the status quo of the last fifty to one hundred years of doing business. Companies that are stuck in the old way of working the supply chain and the old point-of-sale systems will miss out.

Now, it's not only the individual, but it's also the community that is amplifying the change. The key for businesses is to identify how they can tap into communities and provide community experiences. Companies need to understand and engage in the lives of their customer communities.

BRAND TOUCH POINTS

A company personifies itself through its brand. At every touch point, whether it's a call center, a website, or an online forum, a company needs to be listening and communicating.

Consumers increasingly want to positively impact their

communities, their families, and friends. They're not buying the same old corporate communications and marketing. Businesses that bridge the listening gap are learning to tap into the shared consciousness of their potential customers. They are learning to serve the customer and the customer's community before the company. They understand that the customer is their best marketing vehicle. Word of mouth that reaches the community is worth more than advertising because it carries grassroots authenticity.

Procter & Gamble (P&G), for example, has a website called Being Girl. The concept was to create a destination for young, teenage girls. There, girls can explore topics relevant to their age group, anything from dating to acne, menstruation to eating disorders. Experts are available to answer questions, and girls can exchange thoughts and feelings anonymously with one another in open discussion. This type of grassroots community outreach takes place in the marketing arena, and it's available in twenty-five countries.

This new focus is less on pushing a product and more on serving people in their natural communities. Companies that have flipped the old model are listening more as facilitators and enablers. They are developing mechanisms for fostering relationships and putting word-of-mouth communication among peers before advertising. This strategy works.

Being Girl has delivered four times the return on investment (ROI) than traditional marketing. P&G is selling products but selling them passively. At the same time, it is building trust in the brand. Visitors to the site can buy Tampax or Always products, but it's not the main focus of the site. P&G is listening to a community and facilitating relationships within the community. Selling is secondary. First comes understanding the contextual life of teenage girls—what goes on in the individual teenager's mindset and in the shared consciousness of her peer group.

Another example is the online reading and self-publishing community for teenagers called Figment. Hosted by Random House, it's a forum for teens to share and discuss literature and the craft of writing. It facilitates community through chats, forums, newsletters, and even crisis hotlines. With more than 300,000 users, Figment promotes a community of teens built around love of the written word. Of course, by nurturing young readers and writers, Random House builds a market for its books, but the website is not a promotional vehicle for the publisher.

AGE COMMUNITIES

Age groups are natural communities to which we all belong. If we look at age communities from our young adult years onward, we find certain demographic similarities among groups.

The age community of sixteen- to twenty-nine-year-olds, for example, tends to identify with community first and the individual second. In your teens and early twenties, you're trying to figure out who you are and what you like, so you seek out people who are like-minded. They become your cohort and you develop your identities together. Companies that have done a good job matching with this age group tend to put community first as well—companies such as Virgin, Airbnb, Facebook, and Amazon.

As we grow older and mature, we say to ourselves, "I like this, but I don't like that. I've tried this, and I've tried that. This is me, but that's not." From age thirty to fifty-five, the individual matters more. We better know who we are and we're more inclined to assert our individuality. As the individual becomes more focused, community becomes less relevant.

In later life, from fifty-six to eighty, we swing back to community again. We want to feel a deeper sense of belonging, like we're part of something bigger. The individual becomes secondary again to community.

This may all seem like generalization, but it's actually at the heart of society. And smart companies know it. They think about how to approach different age groups. They know demographics count in marketing. They want to know what's important to whom and when, whether it's a community, the individual, or maybe both. They need to know with whom to communicate.

INTEREST COMMUNITIES

When the toy company LEGO began to brainstorm its new product, MINDSTORMS NXT, it knew whom to ask for advice. LEGO went to LUGNET, the largest unofficial community of LEGO fans. LUGNET members have been building elaborately with LEGOs for decades and know the product better than the manufacturer.

LEGO queried LUGNETers about design elements, usability, variations, and possibilities the company itself couldn't envision on its own. The company listened and listened hard. At the same time, LEGO was building an organic community of enthusiasts for its new product. These advisors would become unofficial ambassadors of MINDSTORMS NXT and spread the word.

What I personally love about business is connecting both with individuals and communities. At Samba-Connects, we talk to many different communities with specific shared interests. What they all have in common is the spirit of adventure, which is what SambaConnects is all about. After all, we're in the business of gift experiences. We cater to communities of people who like driving fast cars, skydiving, and whitewater rafting, along with foodies, wine enthusiasts, and other interest communities.

We don't do traditional marketing; we don't advertise. Instead, we cultivate conversation within our interest communities. We engage people we call Sambassadors, who give us street credibility in their communities. These are the folks people listen to. When a Sambassador has an amazing weekend adventure, an excellent dinner, or a thrilling kayaking experience, they communicate on social media with like-minded friends.

We identify Sambassadors as potential influencers by the communication vehicles they use, whether it's video, Instagram, Facebook, Pinterest, or other social media. We invite them to try three experiences a year and share their reactions with their interest community. We have Sambassadors who are bloggers with 50,000 up to 200,000 followers, which is a form of grassroots communication we can't do ourselves. Individuals have a kind of credibility in their communities that companies don't have.

For example, we have a Sambassador who's an extreme adventure seeker. She told us she wanted to do sword fighting, so we hooked her up with a teacher. She posted about her experience in a blog and also posted pictures on Instagram. She was thrilled about the experience and excited to share it.

Mommy bloggers are another example of influencers. These are individuals who choose to reach out on their own to other moms. They've created blogs and websites, such as Savvy Mom, with large audiences who want to know what other moms are feeling and experiencing. They've created their own ecosystems of communication around food, nutrition, health, child raising, and so many other interests that concern them.

Marketing is all about spreading the word, and in the new paradigm of commerce, information sharing among like-minded communities has become a powerful force of localmotion.

CULTURE COMMUNITIES

Back in the day, Apple computers developed its cadre of loyal fans by focusing on innovation, simplicity, and pushing the status quo. Bill Gates and Microsoft invented Windows. Xerox invented the mouse. What Steve Jobs did was put one and one together to create a graphical user interface (GUI) operated by a one-button mouse.

Apple came to market with simplified operation that booted up a smiling happy face with an identifiable sound that personified a new, personalized computer culture. It became Apple culture. Early adopters developed an emotional connection to Apple and hung on tight. They got Apple tattoos and bumper stickers and became a hard-core community of a solid million fans.

But by the late 1990s, Apple had lost its way by introducing too many new products. It'd expanded its customer base of buyers by millions, but only 10 percent of those people were hard-core fans, and Steve Jobs was ousted.

Apple lost its footing, but its die-hard fans held on. Time passed and then Apple entered its renaissance. The company rehired Steve Jobs, and he took the company back to its roots by introducing the iMac. The compact iMac design in customizable colors—blue, red, teal, orange, and purple—challenged the dull, gray boxes of Dell's PCs that required instruction manuals and half a dozen cables to set up. With the iMac, you opened the box, plugged in a single cable, pressed one button, and you were ready to go.

Apple returned to its roots and culture community and continued that innovation through to the iPad and iPhone. In fact, it's broadened that community adding more hard-core followers who gravitate to Apple's culture of innovation and simplicity.

Culture communities coalesce around shared tastes and styles. Musicians, for example, engage their fans not only on an artistic level but also on an emotional level. Dead Heads connected on a deep emotional level with the

Grateful Dead, and it's the same today for Lady Gaga and her Little Monsters. Kanye West, Justin Timberlake, Selena Gomez, and many other pop artists have their own clothing lines. The psychedelic pop band Animal Collective has its own slip-on sneaker designs. Rihanna has her own street-inspired clothing line. Gwen Stefani's L.A.M.B. label is inspired by edgy, punk tastes and design elements reflecting Japanese and Jamaican culture.

These artists are emotionally connecting with fans past the music, developing and extending their brand into their own full-blown, celebrity-community culture. This kind of brand stretching didn't exist until recently. We've entered a new age of cultural artists who are shaping tastes within their communities and extending that emotional connection to other art forms, including fashion and design.

A CAUTIONARY TALE

In the late 2000s, BlackBerry was the number-one-selling smartphone on the market. The shift to Apple occurred quickly after the iPhone was introduced because Apple was able to leverage its customer base and brand promise of superior design and simplicity.

As it turned out, BlackBerry users didn't have the same degree of emotional connection to the company and its products. BlackBerry wasn't able to adapt and connect on a deeper level with its community of users. The company wound up going from a 60 percent market share in 2007 to less than 3 percent ten years later.

It's a cautionary tale for companies to devote themselves to cultivating interest and culture communities around their products or services. The lesson of localmotion is that a business rises or falls on its ability to build its own community of inspired customers.

HOW TO MEET THE NEEDS OF YOUR CUSTOMER COMMUNITY

In the new global marketplace, companies have begun to understand customers as groups of people who share like-minded opinions and tastes. Smart companies are therefore developing products and services to meet the needs of communities.

Millennials care less about owning and more about experience and access. Savvy companies are therefore adjusting their brand touch points, supply chain, and point-of-sale systems to better cultivate and engage millennial customers. Companies are listening more and striving for authenticity in their branding. They have clued in to the group-oriented generation of millennials and are bringing products to market for a generation raised on social media.

Companies are taking their customers' lead by putting relationships before advertising and winning new customers in the process. They are less focused on pushing product and more on serving people in communities through the brand.

Companies that take generational age into account are able to gear their marketing approach to different demographics. At the same time, those companies that pay close attention to the shared interests of different communities can adjust both their product development and fine-tune their marketing to the tastes of specific communities.

Communities coalesce around shared culture and passions. A company that can build a brand around group cultural tastes can build a loyal following. Like-minded communities freely share information, and the new model of marketing is rooted in this information sharing and emotional connection.

Chapter 5

CREATING AN EXPERIENCE

Companies build and connect communities by creating an experience, as opposed to just selling a product or service. Successful companies are consistent and know how to leverage their communications at every touch point. They deliver brand message and brand value at the same time.

eBay started off as an auction site that morphed into a marketing venue for small businesses. In this way, eBay became an enabler delivering value to communities that are interested in certain products, whether it's antiques or leather goods. It's difficult for the small, local seller to reach their market. eBay facilitates the connection and the transaction, but more importantly, it facilitates the experience of community. eBay was initially built around hobbyists and collectors, whether it's knitting, model trains, or guitars, and evolved to virtual storefront sellers.

If you want to buy specialty eyeglasses made in Berlin, you can go to eBay and find several vendors who sell these expensive, handmade brands. They are produced in limited quantities and are difficult to find outside of major cities. But there's a community of people worldwide who wants them and will spend for them.

A competitor of eBay is VarageSale, an online selling venue that was started by a mom on maternity leave. The simple premise is that after the kids grow up and you're left with a bunch of stuff, you can move your garage sale online and reach millions. You supply the goods and VarageSale supplies the buying community.

Online selling venues tap into preexisting communities but also wind up creating new communities. eBay took the local hobbyist to the online world and provided the forum to interact with like-minded people. As eBay developed a critical mass of consumers buying and selling goods, new communities of individuals formed around other consumable goods. The eBay venue actually provides a platform for new relationships around items as obscure as doorknobs, not a traditional collectable. But when you have a platform that can reach billions of people, there are sure to be several hundreds who are looking to sell or buy antique doorknobs. eBay provides the online space, the infrastructure, and marketplace for that community to interact around their passion point.

DELIVERING EXPERIENCE

Unless you're a teenager, you probably haven't heard about Supreme, the skater gear shop that started in New York City in 1994. Supreme created its own brand of accessories catering to the young counterculture of skaters, punks, and "hip-hop heads." It engages artists and designers to create limited editions of merchandise. Supreme will roll out new products on a Thursday and sell out to long lines of buyers. And because there's such a high demand and limited supply, many of those buyers will turn around and resell the shoes or shirts they just bought.

The community itself created a secondary market for Supreme products. There's a large community of Supreme buyers and sellers on eBay, and product demand remains high for even older items. Supreme has keyed into the holy grail of youth culture and delivers on the experience. It has very few retail locations, and each is unique, carrying different, localized inventory. They sell on their own website as well, but the uniqueness of their physical stores and products is something youthful buyers want to experience firsthand. So every Thursday, the lines form for the newest hot items, and by noon the same day, those coveted items appear on eBay.

One of the hottest fashion retailers today is Uniqlo, which is huge in Japan and gaining a strong foothold in Europe. Uniqlo is based on the Gap idea of simple utilitarian clothes for everyday wear: T-shirts and khakis in fifteen color choices. What Uniqlo does that is different, however, is expressed in its name. Each store and its merchandise is unique and curated locally.

Remember the phases of commerce described in chapter 1? In the clothing industry, phase one was to produce mass products cheaply to clothe the masses. You'll find phase one products in shops everywhere and in department stores such as Kroger, Walmart, and Target. Phase two offers a lot more variety in quality and style, including more expensive name brands such as Prada and Dolce & Gabbana, along with the more middle-brow Gap, Banana Republic, and ZARA. In phase three, however, clothing is merchandised more personally and locally. After all, tastes vary from location to location, and people tend to identify with local icons and brands. Remember, phase three trends back to the individual.

Local is therefore becoming the new trend in fashion. It will gradually change the supply chain and shorten the time frame of bringing products to market. Recently,

Uniqlo in London partnered with the United Kingdom's time-honored department store Liberty. As one of the oldest retailers in the world, and originally a fabric company, Liberty has an enormous archive of vintage fabrics, thousands of prints. So Uniqlo is marketing apparel in London made from these vintage fabrics. It wants to sell clothing that is uniquely indigenous to London.

Uniqlo is incentivizing its local stores to partner with local artists and designers, much as Supreme does in New York. Other retailers are doing it, too. H&M is partnering for limited-edition lines with fashion houses such as Balmain and collaborations with celebrities such as retired soccer player David Beckham. What these retailers are doing is marrying the concept of everyday goods to exclusivity and delivering a new experience.

Every product at Uniqlo is durable, simple, affordable, and limited in quantity. You don't have to break the bank to buy it. Its stores in London, Tokyo, and New York are each different and oriented to localized products. The stores are readily identifiable as the Uniqlo brand, but each store's merchandise is adapted to its specific location and community. Not only the merchandise, but also the soundtrack you hear and the scent in the store, each element helps to create a Uniqlo store's own environment. Each is a touch point between the company and its customer community. The stores deliver on the Uniqlo experience.

In the banking industry, which touches almost everyone, perhaps no brand delivers on community experience as well as Umpqua Bank in the western United States. A few years back, the community bank set out from scratch to differentiate itself in the banking marketplace. With an eye on the individuality of communities, the bank's founders decided to create community banks that appealed to their customers' five senses, plus their sense of place.

The design of each bank is therefore unique and community centered, from its architecture and interior design, to soundscape and aromatics. The Umpqua Bank in Portland, Oregon, for example, incorporates a Nirvana music theme in its sound design. It also capitalizes on the city's fame for coffee roasters with the aroma of brewing coffee and the retailing of Umpqua Bank-branded, fair-trade, organic coffee.

Every Umpqua branch pays the same devoted attention to customer service. At the end of every interaction, customers are treated to their choice of a variety of thank-you chocolates. It personifies an organizational commitment to making every banking experience memorable.

In another community-oriented innovation, Umpqua Bank leases meeting space after hours to community groups. Business groups, book clubs, Stitch n' Bitch clubs, all kinds of local groups can reserve space in their local community bank. It's another way that Umpqua Bank is delivering experience.

GIVING BACK

TOMS Shoes has a huge brand following. It's done this by taking the buying experience to a new level of group identity that involves giving. The premise of TOMS is summed up in the company's slogan, "One for One." For every pair of TOMS shoes purchased, the company will donate a pair of shoes to a child in need. What TOMS has done is empower people to help others. It's aligned the brand with comfortable, eco-friendly, fair-trade shoes and social responsibility. Since 2006, TOMS has donated more than sixty million pairs of shoes in more than seventy countries.

TOMS's message is sustainability. The company energizes its customers' group identity through more than a thousand campus clubs. These are dedicated supercommunities who spread the brand message across social channels. Members share pics of themselves wearing TOMS shoes at home and in their travels. The company founder, Blake Mycoskie, set out to create a successful company that could deliver on a charitable service without compromising value.

TOMS has extended the message to fair-trade coffee,

fulfilling a consistent brand promise that provides a meaningful experience for their customers. TOMS Roasting Co. links every coffee purchase to providing safe drinking water to communities worldwide. The company has also extended its brand to eyewear, linking purchases of TOMS Eyewear to eye exams, prescription eyeglasses, and eye surgery in more than a dozen countries.

Whether you're a buyer in New York, San Francisco, London, or Tokyo, you're aware that your TOMS purchase is positively impacting individuals and communities worldwide. As a TOMS customer, you're not only part of the larger TOMS community, but you also come to identify with far-flung communities of kids in Argentina and coffee growers in Guatemala.

This kind of personalization of the buying experience extends the concept of "local" across continents. In the new consumer model, both individuals and communities are looking for companies they can trust. Companies like TOMS are identified with trust, extending their brand by building an impactful consumer culture. It's what the new generation of millennial consumers is looking for. Every shoe sold and every shoe donated has a story. TOMS buyers share their stories with one another, while TOMS shares stories of individuals and communities helped by the TOMS community of giving.

PUBLIC OPINION

Netflix grew by enabling individuals to curate for themselves the movies and shows they want to see. At the same time, Netflix pays close attention to customer selections and tailors its offerings to match customer tastes. It sees customers as communities of people who prefer certain categories of content: action/adventure, romantic comedy, animated sitcom, stand-up comedy. It capitalizes on group tastes by delivering original programming in popular genres with shows such as *House of Cards*, *Orange Is the New Black*, *Sense8*, and *Marco Polo*.

Netflix lets individuals know what's trending and makes suggestions based on an aggregate of people with similar tastes. It actively serves its communities and builds content for groups of viewers. By creating a feedback loop of reviews, it engages individuals in a community dynamic of opinion sharing.

Amazon epitomizes this simultaneous connection to individuals and communities. Its algorithms slice and dice individuals on the basis of shopping and buying habits. It knows what's in your cart and what you've looked at while shopping. When it comes to book selection, which is where the company started, its review system is oriented to the community of readers of particular genres. Readers especially want recommendations; they genuinely want to know what's good and what they should be reading.

When you see a book reviewed by 480 people with a four-and-a-half-star rating, you know it's popular and probably a good read. The details will be in the reviews.

There are also companies that fail to capitalize on public opinion, or worse, they stumble into negative community opinion. Such was the case with Earl's, the casual, fine-dining restaurant chain in Canada. It realized that its customer base was interested in hormone- and antibiotic-free beef, which is a good thing, and it was responsive to its community. Earl's was the first casual-dining chain in Canada to introduce naturally raised beef, and it thought it would be a slam dunk with its customer community.

The mistake Earl's made, however, was it sourced the meat from American-raised cattle because it was cheaper than Canadian beef. It started serving Kansas-raised beef in its sixty-five Canadian restaurants, and there was a big backlash. Earl's loyal customers, all Canadians, started a boycott of the chain because of national pride. They said, "Hey, thanks for bringing in naturally raised beef, but we've got hormone-free cattle raised closer to home right here in Canada." Earl's had listened to its customers, but it hadn't heard the whole story. So it switched to Canadian beef, but the restaurant's still reeling from the boycott, working hard to bring its customer community back into the fold.

Another case of not listening, or not listening carefully

enough, is Schlitz beer. Schlitz wanted to reduce the price of beer and widen its customer base. It did marketing research and focus groups and determined what people liked about the taste, the color, and the packaging. Then Schlitz started tinkering, watering down the beer, adding other ingredients to make it look the same, taste the same, smell the same, seem the same, but the beer wasn't the same, and customers knew it. The company wound up losing its community of Schlitz drinkers.

Coca-Cola brought a similar snafu down on itself when it introduced New Coke. It wanted to compete harder with Pepsi, so it focus-grouped the classic Coke formula, tinkered with it, and to great fanfare introduced New Coke to the market. The community of Coke drinkers immediately rebelled. The company was thrown back on its heels and had to quickly regroup. It managed to save the brand by introducing Classic Coke and rolling back New Coke. Changing the formula was basically shooting itself in the foot. It was disloyalty to the brand's community.

It's one thing to serve the community of Coke drinkers by introducing caffeine-free Coke, low-calorie Zero Coke, Vanilla Coke, or Cherry Coke, as long as the basic Coke taste stays the same. But to pull the classic formula from the market entirely was just crazy. Not many companies can come back from that. Apple came back after it diluted its brand by introducing too many new products that diverged from its core community tastes. Coke also came back. But both companies provide negative lessons of breaking the customer-company bond, the implicit contract that exists with a company's core community.

FAMILY AS COMMUNITY

Disney is a name synonymous with family. What started as the Disney Brothers Cartoon Studio in 1923 is now the multinational mass media Walt Disney Company with film studios, television networks, theme parks, resorts, interactive media, music and theater, merchandising, and consumer products. People generally experience the Disney brand in family groups, whether at a movie theater, a Disney park, a Broadway show, or a Disney resort. Disney speaks to children and adults together. The brand rallies families and fosters relationships, shared experience, and memories.

What Disney does extremely well is that it delivers on touch points where a company and community meet. These touch points are channels of communication, such as social media and mobile phones where information is exchanged. Disney succeeds in a unifying strategy of communication called multichannel. Where it does this best is in its parks. A one- or two-day pass to a Disney theme park comes with Fast Pass, a bracelet that contains all the digital data of your Disney bookings, including rides, entertainment, and any prepaid meals. It's your guide to the park and your total Disney experience with a ride reservation and virtual queuing system. It connects to your handheld device providing maps and guides to attractions, Disney character stories and history, everything that you or your child want to know.

Disney provides the experiences, which are a focal point around which families bond. It's a classic model of personifying a brand. Almost a century after its founding, Disney continues to epitomize a company that connects communities by creating an experience and leveraging communications at every touch point, always building brand value.

MASS CUSTOMIZATION

No company taps the community of children quite like Build-A-Bear. The premise of the business is based on mass customization. For instance, in the clothing industry mass customization involves scanning a person's body measurements, then slightly tailoring precut designs that already approximate the individual's dimensions. Build-A-Bear applied this concept to a popular children's toy—teddy bears. It figured out that not all kids want the same bear. Kids want something soft and cuddly, but with its own unique name, its own color of fur, and the added dimension of watching it get built.

The child begins to establish an emotional connection to their teddy bear right up front. Build-A-Bear went against the grain of mass marketing, which says that you build a product to scale and sell thousands of the same item. Customization, on the other hand, is expensive. Build-A-Bear challenged that by introducing a unique experience that costs more but is well worth it. A child can take a virtual tour with their bear, receive a birth certificate, and customize it to their own local setting.

At Disney World, Build-A-Bear has been extended to Disney characters and toys, such as Build-A-Dino, in its T-Rex Café. The same concept of mass customization applies to American Girl dolls. Instead of one size fits all, American Girls are made to be relatable to girls of many ethnicities and races. They can be personalized to meet the expectations and needs of girls with unique traits or even disabilities. Girls take pictures with their dolls and share them on social media. The dolls are a context for girls to share and relate to their own age and gender community of preteen girls.

Indochino is a specialty brand that mass customizes men's suits at a reasonable price. The company is the largest custom suit maker worldwide. It started as an exclusively online business with the customer sending measurements and choosing material and style. The suits are stitched in Hong Kong or India and shipped to the customer. More recently, Indochino has been opening on-site stores across the United States.

At a time when retail is challenged by online sales, Indochino is expanding past its online strategy to include brick-and-mortar sales. It's a trend that reflects the localization and personalization of the marketplace.

Another example of on-site customization is the Brazilian brand Galibelle, which offers self-styled sandals using an interchangeable system. With stores in fifteen countries from Europe and Africa to Australia and North America, Galibelle offers a unique opportunity for customers to design their own sandals by choosing from a broad selection of soles, straps, and fasteners.

Mass customization will continue to trend and innovate on the world stage as goods and services gain deeper footing in the personalized global marketplace.

REACHING OUT AND BRINGING IN

YouTube is an amazing vehicle to see what a community is like. Individuals with similar interests and passions find common cause and expression on YouTube. There's an entire community called Egg Heads with a passion for barbecuing who swear by the superiority of the Big Green Egg grill. On YouTube, they demonstrate sophisticated techniques for smoking twenty-pound turkeys and briskets. They'll show you how to use the ceramic chamber to make pizza and bake bread. This isn't company driven but rather community driven. Passions coalesce around similar interests, and communities naturally form in the shared environment.

Individuals provide independent video reviews of products as obscure as auto body fillers and like-minded gear heads seek them out. Want to learn how to use Excel software? You'll find demos on YouTube. What begins as a single individual sharing an at-home musical performance can snowball to a following of fans who help launch the career of a Justin Bieber. This wasn't possible before YouTube created a forum for self-expression using video that can reach millions from your living room.

The auto mechanic who shows you how to change a tire on YouTube is engaging an entire global community of people he may never meet. Later, when he demonstrates how to change a car battery or how to check your oil, he's building trust and a following just like a company with a brand to sell. Maybe he's a garage mechanic with a business to promote, and the publicity is beneficial. At the same time, he's building connections among a community with shared interests—people who ask questions and receive answers.

ENGAGING HEARTS AND MINDS

Forward-thinking companies from manufacturers to restaurants are learning to find the touch points to connect with their customers as communities. What it takes is to deliver a valuable experience that's memorable. This is how companies that embrace the new consumer model are engaging hearts and minds around brands, such as TOMS Shoes and Uniqlo clothes.

With the advent of the IoT and the ability of the internet to engage people in new forms of collaboration, the old ways of doing business are falling away. Old-school companies such as airlines have to learn to engage their customer communities at every touch point, from ticket buying, to the service counter, to seating, to food, to the call center. Every level of customer-company contact has to carry an experience of service both to the individual and the collection of individuals who form the company's natural community. Every touch point of customer-company contact is an opportunity and has to deliver to the customer-community experience.

Online sellers need to ask themselves: Is my website user friendly? Can the customer readily access information? Do we truly understand our target community of customers? Do we provide quick access for answers to questions? Does our customer service truly serve customer needs? Is our shipping and returns policy customer friendly? Do we enable customer interaction? And most importantly: Are we providing positive, memorable experiences of our product or service?

These are the points that distinguish a good brand from a bad brand, a successful company from a failing company.

HOW TO MAKE YOUR BRAND VALUES
= COMMUNITY VALUES

Successful companies know how to leverage communication. They put more emphasis on building a brand community than on selling a product or service. They tie the value of their brand with their message. They build both their brand and their brand community around passion points.

Companies do this by tapping into existing communities and also by creating new communities that share a passion for the brand. Individuals in communities want to actually experience the brand, not just buy it or use it.

In the shift toward local, communities are coalescing around local tastes in fashion and culture. Youthful buyers want what is unique and locally curated. This extends from clothing to music, to community banking.

Community-oriented people also want to give back. They are active on social media and value sustainability, so they seek out brands with social consciousness. They think globally and act locally. They are looking for meaningful experiences in the service of communities across boundaries.

This new consumer model is built on trust. Communities have expectations for their preferred brands and expect them to deliver. Brand value is built and reinforced at every touch point wherever information is shared. Community-driven brands know how to reach out and bring in. They create a messaging environment that supports the values that their brand community holds dear.

Delivering memorable brand experiences is what draws communities in. Therefore, every touch point, whether online, on smartphone, or at in-store locations, has to deliver on the brand experience. Websites need to be user friendly, questions need ready answers, customer service should be all about service. Every interaction needs to reflect positively on the brand and the values of community associated with the brand.

Chapter 6

CREATING A TRIBE

The company that is probably the granddaddy of community builders is Harley-Davidson motorcycles. When Harley-Davidson went public on the New York Stock Exchange, instead of ringing the bell as is usually done, a group of big bearded guys with leather vests and bandanas rode their Harley "hogs" onto the trading floor and revved their engines. Harley is more than a brand to them; it's their tribe.

Harley-Davidson has its own culture and way of life. Its focus is on authenticity and the experience of freedom, right down to the distinctive rumble of a Harley. The company sponsors Harley Owners Group, HOG clubs that pretty much define what's come to be called the subculture of consumption. Every dealership sponsors its own club, and HOG members spend considerably more on Harley merchandise and events than other Harley owners.

Harley represents a trifecta of the brand, the individual, and the community, which together are the tribe. Tribal brand identity is more intense than the usual community experience fostered by a brand. Tribalism occurs on the organic level of individuals forming community on their own. A company can tap that community, connect to it, encourage it, and create a fertile environment for it, but the tribe creates itself.

Through the years, Harley has kept its following by never diluting its brand. For example, it manufactures a separate line of sport bikes to compete with Japanese bikes but not under the Harley name. Other brands have had loyal followings. Corvette had a strong nostalgic brand, but it failed to consistently deliver on the brand experience. When brands deviate from community expectations, they lose their community. Once a brand has established a strong community base, that community has to be nurtured. Apple lost its way through its own expansion but turned around in time to hold its core of dedicated zealots.

TRIBAL SPORTS

When England plays in the World Cup of football (soccer), local churches will bring in TVs if the match falls on a Sunday. In the global arena of football, team tribal identity is so strong that fans have to sit in different stadium sections. At the Euro 2016 match, Russian and English fans brawled in the streets of Marseille. Hundreds of French police had to use tear gas to disperse them.

Steelers Nation isn't just Pittsburgh or western Pennsylvania; it's a tribal football culture that extends to sports bars as far afield as San Diego, California, and Phoenix, Arizona. There's a Pittsburgh Bar and Restaurant in North Belfast, Ireland, and a Steelers fan base in Shanghai, China. Steelers Nation has outposts in Monterrey, Mexico, as well as Kuwait and Italy.

The intensity of the team's identity can't be explained by brand promotion or advertising. It's been fostered by collective history, family association handed down from father and mother to son and daughter. The Pittsburgh Steelers organization can run with it, they can partner with the National Football League (NFL) to sell merchandize and cash in on it, but team tribalism is born of cultural dynamics that go deeper than the team itself to shared history, even class identity. Of course, the merchandize doesn't hurt. Those authentic NFL jerseys with player names emblazoned on the back help drive the tribe, but nothing fosters the tribe more than actual wins on the field and championship rings.

FOOD, POLITICS, AND RELIGION

In England, celebrity chef Jamie Oliver has more than

600,000 subscribers who are trying to help him reform government policy by driving awareness around healthy eating. An affable and self-deprecating TV personality and restaurateur, Oliver has built a tribal brand around simplicity, organic foods, and humanely raised animals. Through the strength of his commitment, cooking talents, and charisma, he's managed to tap into an organic tribe of health-conscious foodies who were ready to embrace his mission of change around what we eat.

On the distinctly political front, the 2016 US presidential election saw a coalescing of natural tribes around candidates professing values and policies that defined distinct communities. Supporters of Bernie Sanders "felt the Bern" with a tribal passion around issues of income equality, access to higher education, and getting the big money out of politics. Meanwhile, blue-collar workers who felt abandoned by the new global economy rallied around their own candidate of change, the billionaire Donald Trump, who promised to "Make America Great Again" for the middle and working classes. Each tribe was a collection of individuals united to support their candidate and their own shared values with the passion of acolytes.

Of course, the term acolyte usually refers to religious followers. Tribes through history have been associated with family, clan, ethnic, and religious groups. These are the roots of our tribal identities. In the social arena and marketplace, we transfer those tribal tendencies to other identities of association, whether it's a motorcycle brand, a football or soccer team, a political candidate, food consciousness, or, as we'll see next, the tribal culture of gaming.

MASSIVE GAMING

In the world of gaming, tribes coalesce around massively multiplayer, online games (MMOG), such as World of Warcraft and Clash of Clans. These "open-world" games immerse players in interactive competition, cooperation, and role-playing in virtual environments across internet platforms. Tribal subcultures of players pay monthly fees to join communities, such as Sony's PlayStation, to gain access.

Clash of Clans is a newer top-grossing, app-based game in which players become virtual members of clans that engage in warfare. Players create alliances among competing clans and hone their skills. Open virtual worlds like World of Warcraft require total immersion for long periods, hours of play creating characters and alter egos. Dwarfs, elves, and barbarians go adventuring to find opportunities and riches in worlds of magic and mayhem. Players bond with other players across continents from North America to Africa. People who've never met in person find common cause in a field of play with its own social structures.

MMOGs tap into basic human instincts for community with like-minded people. Games like World of Warcraft are so technically immersive that players form compelling emotional bonds. It is so popular that it spawned a film in 2016 that grossed more than $430 million worldwide.

Activision's Call of Duty immerses players in more modern virtual warfare. It's a blockbuster with a strong tribal following across many iterations of the game, beginning with World War II and followed by more contemporary settings such as Modern Warfare and Black Ops.

Ease of access to MMOGs, whether on a desktop or Xbox, a smartphone or iPad, facilitate the formation of tribes around the games. The companies behind these games don't actually create the tribes. What they create is the product around which tribes can form organically on their own. It's similar to the dynamic at play with Harley-Davidson HOGs.

In sports, food, and politics, tribes rally to a team, a cause, or a lifestyle that taps into strong feelings of emotional connection. Marketers can't force people into groups. Great brands don't push people; all they can do is facilitate and enable a community to flourish.

THE APPEAL OF LULULEMON

Lululemon's business model of technical athletic ware, primarily for women and primarily for yoga, taps into a preexisting tribal community of physical enthusiasts. Free yoga classes and in-store events, festivals, and retreats provide the context for community association. Lululemon appeals to a shared sensibility for well-designed athletic attire that is produced using sustainable practices.

Lululemon stores become hubs for local tribes that value healthy lifestyles. Sweat with Us events and classes such as Authentic Living and Mindfulness nurture the tribe. Of course the company's endgame is to sell its products, but the path it takes to get there is centered on local community. Lululemon products are sold only by Lululemon, not by other distributors, as is the case with Nike, Adidas, and Under Armour. It's more like the Apple model of exclusivity, and this reinforces the tribe. For the tribe, it's more than a product; it's an experience of connection and deeper meaning.

LET'S MEETUP

Tribalism occurs when a group of individuals with mutual interest connects to a focal point such as a product or idea. It is something of a mutual discovery.

In this sense, Meetup groups represent the epitome of

social tribalism. Meetup is basically a network of more than nine thousand local groups that initially connect through an online social networking portal. Each group comes together locally in real time and physical places around similar interests or activities. These are natural communities: running clubs, singles clubs, entrepreneurs, artists, book lovers.

Meetup is exclusively about shared connection to others. There is no product, no sell, nothing to market. There is only community, shared time, and space.

TAKING THE BULL BY THE HORNS

At the other extreme, and I do mean *extreme*, is a product that taps a preexisting tribe. The energy drink Red Bull targets a youthful community of extreme sports enthusiasts who live a daring lifestyle. The drink fuels the lifestyle.

Red Bull sponsors speed skating, Grand Prix motorcycle racing, Formula One racing, off-road motorsports, and extreme water sports. It encourages online sharing of GoPro videos that show extreme accomplishments: cliff diving, entering a volcano, surfing in high waves. Red Bull is both the fuel and the home of a youthful tribe that's trying to push the physical limits. For example, the company sponsored an extreme jumper equipped with an oxygen mask and custom gear who jumped from the outer reaches of the Earth's atmosphere.

In this way, the product associates itself with an existing tribe and promotes itself and the tribe at the same time. Red Bull sells more than a drink; it sells adventure and pushing the limits. It is savvy enough to engage at all the touch points from online forums to music festivals.

Red Bull sponsors events worldwide from Lollapalooza and AFROPUNK in the United States to Gamescom and Red Bull Heroicks in Germany, Red Bull Dragon War in Hong Kong, and Red Bull Beat Battle in Russia. It sponsors the Red Bull Clásico de Vitilla in New York City, a baseball-like sport played with a plastic bottle cap and a broomstick that originated in the Dominican Republic. Red Bull makes it its business to be everywhere and go everywhere the tribe goes.

PLAYING WITH THE BAND

Tribes have been coalescing around music probably since the birth of music itself. In traditional societies, music is deeply associated with group ritual and worship. In popular culture and entertainment, music plays a different role, but it still moves people individually and collectively. In popular music, fans sometimes do coalesce as tribes, and perhaps no band epitomizes this more than the Grateful Dead.

Deadheads coalesced in the 1960s as dedicated followers of the band's music. They attended concerts religiously and many followed the band on tour. The hippie-like culture of Deadheads endured way past the hippie era and the tribe endured for decades across generations.

Some of this same dedication to a band and a musical art form extends to fans of the Rolling Stones, Depeche Mode, and U2. For contemporary musicians who seek a fan base, it's bands like these with strong tribal adherents that represent the model of success so many still strive for in popular music.

TAPPING THE TRIBE

Today, with the prevalence of social media, online communication, and short attention spans, tribal connections among like-minded people are becoming even more important. Companies compete for attention. They try to tap public interest through Facebook, Twitter, and websites and are disappointed when they come up empty. What they are missing is the kind of relevance and emotional connection that speaks to a tribe.

Companies need to ask themselves: Who are the like-minded people we are trying to reach? How do we tap into an existing community and enable the tribe to interact?

How is it that Harley-Davidson has done such a great job of coalescing a tribe around a transportation machine when other automotive companies have failed?

The answer may lie with the new automotive paradigm of Tesla. Tesla hit the ground running as an innovative auto company busy building prototypes of electric and self-driving cars. It's a phase three company that taps into an existing community of drivers who care about sustainable energy and society's overreliance on fossil fuels. Tesla represents not only disruptive technology but also a disruptive marketing model of direct-to-consumer sales with no middlemen. The company is driven by the same worldview shared by its customers. It's an innovative car company responding to the challenges of our times. It doesn't have to seek out its customers. Presale orders of Tesla's new Model 3 are upward of 400,000 buyers. They are a tribe in waiting, the leading edge of motorists waiting to turn the key on their electric vehicles. They're a new breed of Tesla motor heads.

In Canada, another paradigm shift has occurred in the world of telecommunications. For a long time now, three companies have dominated the Canadian telecommunications market—Bell, Telus, and Rogers. However, they're generally not liked. Cable fees are high and mobile phone fees are among the highest in the world. Along came Wind Mobile (now called Freedom Mobile) in 2008 with a new concept of affordable wireless service on a no-contract basis.

Wind Mobile quickly changed the Canadian telecommunications landscape by targeting youth with a grassroots approach that tapped a collective frustration about the old way of doing things. It quickly became the country's fourth largest provider with 800,000 subscribers. Customers pay lower monthly fees with no years-long contracts. Wind Mobile's disgruntled tribe was actually out there waiting for them. It could have been anyone, any telco company with the right concept, but Wind Mobile got there first, and others will likely follow.

In the marketplace, successful companies always fulfill an existing need for a product or service. The need may not always be definable beforehand, but when the right product hits the market, it becomes obvious that the need was there. The same concept holds for tribes. When a product touches a common chord among many, a natural customer community responds. If the emotional connection to the product goes deep enough, that community responds with the fervor of a tribe in the grips of localmotion.

HOW TO CONNECT TO YOUR TRIBE

The appeal of a brand to a community of customers reaches its peak when that community identifies as a tribe. Tribes have their own culture and way of life defined by their relationship to the brand. The tribe comprises individuals who are passionate about and identify with the brand. Companies need to be responsive and connect to, encourage, and nurture their tribe. But the tribe creates itself.

Companies that want to keep their tribe can never dilute or deviate from the brand. They must meet their tribe's expectations for the brand. This kind of tribal affiliation involves cultural dynamics and emotional connections such as the kind that occurs with team sports. It can be passed down from generation to generation and can involve shared history.

Tribes can be organized around shared values and common goals, whether about lifestyle, food, politics, music, religion, or other social or cultural tastes. When a product touches a common chord, a natural customer community responds. If the emotional connection goes deep enough, the community responds with the fervor of a tribe. There are tribal subcultures in the worlds of gaming, yoga, automobiles, and fashion.

Tribes can coalesce around an existing product, but there are times when a new product connects to an already existing tribe. This is the case with certain products that appeal to extreme sports enthusiasts who may connect to a product that fuels and endorses their lifestyle.

Companies compete for attention and try to tap public interest on social media. The right product or service can appeal to existing communities and sometimes generate tribal connection when a product has strong relevance and emotional appeal. Products that fill an existing need and foster interaction between customer and brand stand the best chance.

The need may not always be clear beforehand, but when the right product hits the market, it becomes obvious the need was there. That's the recipe for connection to the shared interests and passions of a tribe.

THE TECHNOLOGY

Chapter 7

SOCIAL MEDIA

The essence of social media is digital communication. Whether it's blogging, Twitter, YouTube, image sites such as Pinterest, messaging applications such as WhatsApp, or community and friend-sharing sites such as Facebook, social media relies on digital environments. Social media platforms cast huge nets that impact localmotion in two ways:

First, social media enables the individual to create their own voice and message.

Second, social media enables both individuals and communities to connect with many people around similar interests.

It's important for companies to use social media well, which means using platforms selectively. A business should tailor its social media strategy to its product, service, and corporate agenda. Twitter may be ideal for one company but not another. The same goes for Facebook or Google+. When considering social media strategy, a company should look at five proof points, or tenets.

FIVE TENETS OF SOCIAL MEDIA

1. Respond quickly: Whether you're on Pinterest or Facebook, if you take too long to respond, you don't get engagement. Slow response time shows that you don't care as a company.
2. Be authentic and real: Customers can detect a disconnect between real and made-up conversations. Flashy ads and hype don't resonate on social media where expectations are high for genuine communication.
3. Be committed: Social media isn't something that can be done in dribs and drabs. It requires daily involvement.
4. Choose the right channels: Tailor your social media communications to the channels that best suit your product or service.
5. Be local: Companies that engage socially through a local lens will have greater impact. Local is where the future is going. Companies can engage with multiple audiences across different geographies, but it still must be done in a local context.

AUTHENTIC LOCAL CONNECTION

In an age when radio is a very competitive and crowded field, trying to attract a customer audience is very difficult. Yet upstart Toronto radio station Indie88 successfully found its audience and relatively quickly. The station started online with an interactive website and a very simple premise: authentic, indie rock with a strong, local flavor. Unlike mainstream stations that are wrapped up in advertising, Indie88 began by leveraging its local connections to promote breakout bands and penetrate the local market.

The station began streaming online in April 2016, and the first song was Arcade Fire's "Wake Up." It was like a siren song for a new station that wanted to align itself with emerging artists not signed to any label, indie or otherwise. Indie88 committed a large portion of its format hours to local programming, and at the same time it curated indie music from around the world. The format and premise is driven by listener engagement.

Indie88 has a very successful social media strategy that uses Facebook, Twitter, Instagram, Flickr, and photo blogs extremely well. It uses social media to connect with customers and musicians in a format that has particular appeal to millennials who are always looking for the newest and hippest thing. Indie88 highlights Canadian musicians but also plays indie music from as far afield as Finland.

The station initiated a market-savvy Superfriends program that encourages individual fans to communicate with the larger fan base about parties, excursions, and road trips related to concert tours. Superfriends are die-hard fans—the biggest listeners who follow a band closely. When a band is launching a new concert tour or album, Indie88 engages the band's Superfriends to disseminate social media messages. A listener who is streaming music on the Indie88 website sees various links, information, and updates on their favorite band's touring schedule or new release.

At the same time, the station offers giveaways. This functions as an engagement tool that drives Indie88 listenership. If you're not an active listener and not on Facebook or Twitter, it's difficult to access shows and concerts. The Superfriends program drives customer awareness wrapped around fan-base loyalty. It's a very compelling way to get customers to talk about Indie88 in the context of their favorite musical artists. In a very short time frame, the station has grown a loyal following of listeners and expanded its influence. At the same time, it is giving a leg up to independent musicians who are trying to reach an audience.

What Indie88 has done really well is to become a distribution point for independent artists who are below the radar of mainstream stations. For a product or service, the bottom line is distribution. Indie88 is like a local college station with a professional vibe. It's a new breed of radio station that engages individuals and community members in social interactions that bring listeners closer to the indie musicians they love. By building distribution around social media, Indie88 has created a win-win for artists, the station, and fans of indie music.

BRAIN GAME

One of the top ten board games right now is Cranium, the brain-testing game that has breathed new life into a time-honored form of gaming. Cranium has taken board-gaming mainstream again. The game, which combines elements of charades and Pictionary with brain-testing questions, is played by two-person teams. Each couple is asked a variety of questions that test their knowledge. What's truly innovative, however, is how this small game company is using social media to engage people in further developing the game.

The company interacts with consumers in unique ways on Twitter and Facebook. It posts trivia questions and puzzles daily and engages people in Guess This Tune, or gets them to watch a video and respond. The company actively encourages people to devise new questions, and by doing so, it is creating communities around Cranium, getting people to invest their time and energy in the game.

This participation in game development builds a sense of ownership, along with social and personal investment. With every version of Cranium that comes out, there's a good chance players will recognize their own contribution.

At the company level, the game's developers have created something of an ongoing focus group that vets questions. Game developers can see which questions really resonate with players and use that feedback to improve their product. With this ongoing community involvement, Cranium is building consistency, which is essential to any brand. The company draws people into the very premise of the product, and by tying it all together on social media, Cranium's developers are simultaneously engaging players and improving the game.

If you're on Facebook playing a Cranium-initiated quiz or puzzle and you're not already a Cranium player, you may very well soon be. It's a great way to bring people into the fold, because games are built around shared social experience. Social media is therefore an ideal environment for tying virtual play to the actual board game, which occurs in the physical world. It's an amazing marketing dynamic that never existed until now.

EXPERIENCE MORE: LIVE *MÁS*

Taco Bell is an old-school, fast food chain designed for

mass consumption. It's what we defined in the early chapters as a phase one company—not what anyone would consider local. Yet Taco Bell has been shifting its brand mindset via social media with new likability and humor. The company's social media posts are relatable and not pitchy. Taco Bell isn't saying, "Try our product"; instead, it's building authenticity. And the way to do it is by engaging customer feedback and participation.

Taco Bell has ten million Facebook fans and 1.7 million followers on Twitter. Customers are also messaging about the company on Snapchat and other platforms. The company is listening and reacting instantaneously, which is no easy task. Taco Bell scours the internet for what people are saying about its products. Customers are tweeting and sharing messages about Taco Bell all the time. They use Instagram to show what they're currently eating, and the company encourages it. Taco Bell asks people to message on Snapchat about what they're doing right in the moment. The company will intercept a discussion, jump in and retweet, or reply and offer comments.

Through engagement on social media, Taco Bell has become an active participant in the conversation about its brand. It introduces new menu items in creative ways in the social media environment. What Taco Bell has clued into is the trend of millennials to value experience above anything else. Millennials want to dialogue about the products they use, and they want to take products to the next level. When Taco Bell responds in the moment to a tweet or post, millennials love it. When someone posts a Facebook video of himself skateboarding while eating a burrito, Taco Bell reposts it. That's instant attention and reward for a cool move that ten million people see on Facebook. Taco Bell rides that video clip with a social media message about keeping it real and living life to the fullest, which dovetails with the company's slogan: Live *Más*.

DO THE DEW

Another old-school, one-trick pony that has changed its face on social media is Mountain Dew. In 2010, PepsiCo, which owns and produces Mountain Dew, created a social media campaign called DEWmocracy to engage consumers in suggesting new flavors. The campaign fostered social media interactions, asking people to post their suggestions on Twitter. DEWmocracy also solicited ideas for new bottle designs, and local artists posted drawings. It was all about creating a new culture around Mountain Dew that didn't involve traditional advertising.

The brand wanted people to "Do the Dew" in new and entertaining ways. It encouraged posts depicting activities associated with drinking Mountain Dew. DEWmocracy was all about participation and creativity. The company would message, "These are the three flavors we're thinking about. What do you guys think?" It was a clever way to launch a social media campaign by making the product more relevant to millennials. This kind of social engagement builds on itself, as friends tell friends and the dialogue expands to a wider fan base.

DORITOS did something very similar. The brand engaged millennials on social media with the DORITOS Challenge to reimagine the product. It was a very compelling way to reframe an old-school product that isn't particularly local or good for you. Yet it captured the social imagination of a community that likes to be engaged.

Nowadays when old-line consumer products such as Mountain Dew and DORITOS run digital ads, they do it more to reinforce new social media campaigns than to brazenly sell. The messaging is more like, "Hey, go to our Facebook page and give us your opinion on DORITOS Fire Sriracha chips." It's all about soliciting engagement.

MIRACLES ON SOCIAL MEDIA

WestJet is an innovative Canadian airline, second only to Air Canada, that is engaging customers and employees in new ways. WestJet employees actually own shares in the company, which gives them more of a stake in the company's success. WestJet also provides 24-7 social media support for customers. Wherever customers are in the world, they can engage with the airline on Twitter or Facebook to get the information they need. That is a very big deal because it avoids the hassle and wait times of old-school customer service calls.

WestJet goes the extra mile in building community. In 2013, it launched a social media campaign called Christmas Miracle to promote random acts of kindness. The company's goal was to motivate its employees around the world to promote and submit mini miracle videos via social media channels. Employees posted two thousand small snippets of unscripted, authentic video with emotional warmth. It drove home a strong sense that the company and its employees really care about people.

Christmas Miracle was so popular on social media channels that it wound up becoming a launch pad for the airline's new advertising campaign. Unlike typical ad campaigns, WestJet started at the grassroots level reaching out to individuals and communities. This magnified the impact of the company's message, while helping to personalize the brand and set it apart from the competition. The company ended up winning a social media Shorty Award.

The Christmas Miracle campaign has become a yearly staple, generating increased interest and participation every holiday season. Since 2013, the campaign has generated some forty-four million video views. Its broad appeal is based on authenticity. The campaign is heartfelt, unscripted, and local. Videos are of real people in real time doing good deeds, which resonate especially well around the holiday season. It's a hugely successful campaign that follows the tenets of social media engagement.

SPRAY IT ON PINTEREST

Facebook and Twitter get a lot of attention on social media, but sometimes nothing beats Pinterest for live action. When the spray paint company Krylon wanted to engage an audience for its brand of high-bonding, nonchip paint, it decided to create a stir on Pinterest. Company staff members took to the road logging seven hundred miles across the United States going to yard sales and purchasing more than one hundred items. They then transformed those items with Krylon paint, sold them on Pinterest for double what they'd spent, and donated the money to charity.

What happened is the company's following on Pinterest increased by 400 percent in just a few weeks. The overall budget for the project was $200,000, and it delivered $2.7 million in earned media. Then Krylon invited its Pinterest followers to transform their own garage sale items with Krylon paint. The company invited people to spray paint items they wanted to sell and to share their handiwork on Krylon's Pinterest page. Customers videotaped themselves refurbishing everything from bicycles to furniture.

Krylon made it interesting by engaging people in a sort of show-and-tell kind of spray painting demo. Pinterest is great for capturing imagery, and people went ahead and posted their garage sales. They'd show some old bike getting a Krylon paint makeover in real time. It was all very cool and generated huge interest in the activity. It wound up building relevancy for the product that didn't exist before. In the growing DIY social environment, Krylon came along at just the right time.

WORKBRAIN HIRING

Just a few years back, companies relied almost exclusively on references. Now they are turning to social media both for recruitment and as a way of screening applicants. Firms are looking to see how applicants communicate on social media, what they post, whom they talk to, and what their pictures look like. An individual's social media trail is all public knowledge, so there's nothing inherently wrong in accessing that information; it's all aboveboard. Social media has entered the realm of hiring.

This new hiring environment opened the door to Workbrain, an HR recruitment company that offers social media screening for employers. Instead of a company's HR department having to do social media research themselves, they hire it out to the experts at Workbrain. It's a valuable resource for employers looking for the right hires. Companies are looking to minimize risk, and they'll use every resource at their disposal to screen for candidates who fit their company culture. They want to know how a person spends their time, what their interests are, what they do on weekends. Rightly or wrongly, social media is a window into the individual. It's a profoundly different world we live in now, where privacy has become very fluid.

OWNING YOUR SPACE

American Express distinguishes itself from other credit cards by actually "talking" to its audience. Unlike Visa and Mastercard, which work through many different banks, Amex has the advantage of being its own bank and its own brand. It's a credit card company that owns its own space and has extended its brand with social media.

American Express uses Twitter and Facebook to provide context and forums for exclusive deals and front-of-the-line passes. Cardholders want to know: How can I redeem my points? How long will it take me to earn points and flight miles? What's the difference in earnings between gold and platinum cards?

By virtue of exclusive offers, American Express carries a certain distinction and cachet beyond the mainstream. Only cardholders can enter the running for select concert tickets or special deals on merchandise. Access can mean everything, and social media is a perfect platform for enhancing access. Through the spontaneity of social media, American Express can loop customers in, start the conversation, listen, and respond.

American Express partners with other brands and industry associations in business-to-business (B2B) partnerships. For example, the company might send a tweet saying, "Beginning at 8:00 p.m. tonight, cardholders can purchase tickets in this exclusive offer," or invite participation with a tweet such as, "Hey, if you want to see Justin Bieber on opening night, send the funniest tweet about why you want to go." It's a heads-up that confers special status to the loyal customer. This is why so many big acts and major brands, such as Warner Brothers, Universal Records, and Virgin, partner with American Express. Everyone, including the consumer, is enhanced by the association.

COMMERCE IN THE FUTURE MOMENT

The future of social media will increasingly involve communication and commerce in the immediate moment. Social media is already bridging the gap, connecting conversation and point of purchase. Facebook isn't a great commerce site yet, but at some point, it will be. Pinterest is a social media tool, but it's already becoming a great commerce site because people can pin their interests and the products they see.

This happened to my wife recently. She was out shopping and became interested in a jacket that was on sale. It was the last one and it fit her, but she wasn't quite sure about buying it. She wanted another opinion, so she messaged a photo of the jacket to friends, asking, "Do you like this jacket?"

Companies will be jumping on this dynamic more and more. Artisans are always cluing into new venues for distribution. Pinterest introduced Buyable Pins in 2015 linking up sales with sellers' Shopify pages. Local sellers are pinning merchandise, and buyers are responding. Facebook won't be far behind once it gets its act together for commerce. Facebook started out with likes, then shifted to capturing moments and sharing things. Commerce is sure to follow because social media is in constant flux.

At its baseline, social media connects the individual to the community and the community to the individual. Platforms connect buyers to sellers, and businesses to other businesses—both large and small. Social media thrives on interaction, bettering lives through communication, while continually seeking authenticity in personal and community connections, and in the products we buy.

HOW TO USE SOCIAL MEDIA

Social media platforms cast huge nets. They enable individuals to create their own message and share their own voice. They also enable communities to connect around similar interests. Opportunities to capture the popular imagination abound on social media. Businesses therefore need to use social media selectively to communicate about their brand.

Engagement on social media brings companies to the community conversation. Social engagement allows for company expression of brand culture beyond the confines of traditional advertising. It builds dialogue and widens the fan base, especially among the generation of millennials who value experience above all else. Social media platforms allow for clever ways to launch campaigns to make a product or service more relevant.

Companies can engage successfully on social media by following five core tenets:

1. Respond quickly: Fast response shows that you care.

2. Be authentic and real: People respond to genuine messaging.

3. Be committed: Stay involved every day.

4. Choose the right channels: Tailor your messaging.

5. Be local: The local context has the best impact.

Companies can foster participation and creativity by encouraging consumers to interact with the brand. Customers welcome opportunities to respond in the moment with a tweet or a post to share their impressions. Engagement of this kind personalizes the brand and sets it apart from the competition. Genuine and unscripted interaction generates interest and builds relevancy for the product. Social media will continue to grow and expand as a vehicle for commerce.

Social media is a window into the company and a window into the community of customers. It opens access and loops customers into the conversation, listening, initiating, and responding. It can readily connect customers to the point of purchase and facilitate commerce in the immediate moment.

Chapter 8

APPS, AI, AND THE IOT

Artificial intelligence is the driving force behind localmotion. AI is constantly shaping how individuals connect with products and services. At the same time, AI is driving connectivity and enabling the internet of things. In our new world of IoT, devices embedded with software can be sensed and controlled remotely across personalized networks. AI is all about predictability and algorithms applied to driverless cars, climate control in our homes, our music apps, and our buying decisions online.

These are the growth engines of the new global economy. Companies that understand and integrate IT and AI are reaping the rewards of our new marketplace. AI is making it easier for companies to know the individual consumer. At the same time, AI is enabling consumers to select and buy products and services more easily.

APPS, THE GREAT ENABLER

Software applications or programs, commonly called apps, are enabling our lives. Apps run on computers and the internet, but most people associate apps with smartphones and other mobile devices. This is primarily because Apple popularized downloadable apps for the iPhone and quickly became a dominant player in the mobile device field.

Apps are software tools that enable users to do any number of things: keep track of their health, listen to music, access bus schedules, and so much more. Applications allow individuals to customize what is most relevant to them personally, depending on what they like to eat, where they live, or how they commute.

Smartphone penetration in the population is ubiquitous across generations. Almost everybody has one. Apps are at the heart of localmotion because they empower people to communicate more effectively and efficiently. Software applications enable businesses to reach past small and medium-sized markets.

Until recently, larger businesses always had the edge in moving products across wider markets. What apps have done is facilitate a transition from top-down marketing to bottom-up. Local and community players have been empowered like never before to reach broader audiences for their products and services. At the same time, it is consumers themselves at the local ground level who adopt the apps they like and make them go mainstream.

FROM THE GROUND UP

Companies such as Facebook, Google, and Apple are the new General Motors, Fords, and GEs of the world. Facebook started at the local level in a university and later took the world by storm. As evidenced by indicators such as the S&P and NASDAQ, tech companies are continually changing the marketplace. Technology translates into sheer market power because tech firms are constantly innovating in an arena of connecting individuals and communities.

A perfect example is Waze, the largest community-based traffic and navigation app in the world. It started out in 2006 as a community project called FreeMap Israel and was acquired by Google in 2013 for $1.1 billion.

The application uses GPS and driver-submitted data about routes and travel time to track local traffic patterns. It's a perfect confluence of locally based information contributed by individuals and shared by the community. Waze collects data from individual users to build algorithms and generate information back to the aggregate of local travelers. In this way, it is essentially crowdsourced mapping.

Waze was able to outshine both Google Maps and Apple Maps by being a better application than both of them. The appeal of Waze is due to its superior analytics. It simply does more for people. Waze empowers users to travel effectively according to immediate traffic conditions and movement patterns. The application's traffic-flow algorithms disseminate the most up-to-date data on viable routes.

As a downloadable application, Waze isn't only the best GPS out there; it also provides the best path from point A to point B in real time. There's never been a product that has come even close to Waze. It tracks everything from accident reports, traffic jams, and police traps to landmarks, house numbers, and the cheapest fuel available on route.

The latest innovation in Waze is to provide incentives to engage users and encourage them to provide more information. Waze uses gaming conventions, such as dropping digital cookie crumbs and cupcakes for drivers to earn points by following the best routes to keep traffic flowing. In this way, it can encourage travel along certain routes, sometimes to test if the route is more viable, or to push a quicker and safer route. The payoff for the individual can be a faster commute, saving gas, or just the good feeling of contributing to the community of travelers.

Another application, called Citymapper, uses public transportation data. It pulls information from various users of buses and trains, bicycles, taxicabs, and Uber rides to help individuals get from place to place more efficiently. Citymapper provides the user with options for public travel. It started in London and is now in twenty-nine cities. Citymapper's motto is, "We want a big city to feel like a little village." It's a great utilitarian product.

When I was traveling in Tokyo fifteen years ago, I used a very early version of a similar app on a PalmPilot. It helped me navigate a subway system in which all the signs were in Japanese.

Citymapper is now hugely successful for navigating large urban centers around the world. It appeals to travelers or anyone who's new to a major city and needs help getting around. It reduces much of the worry and anxiety about travel in a foreign city. It's exciting to fly to new destinations, but without an app like Citymapper, a visitor can spend considerable time and energy researching how to get around once they get there. The app provides real-time data that makes travel easier and wait times shorter.

Citymapper got me out of a mess when I was in London about two years ago. I had literally just downloaded the app and I was using it for the first time. I'd arrived in London and had an interview in the East End near Liverpool Street station. As it turned out, there was a huge rainstorm, and for the first time in fifty years, the London Underground was flooded. The only way to travel was by bus, and Citymapper saved my hide. It told me something like, "Walk 300 meters, turn right, go to this bus stop, take the number 52 bus," and so on. It directed me to change for another bus, and I made it to my destination. That's the power of AI.

CALLING THE TUNE

Listener access to music has changed over the last twenty years, from CDs to digital downloads, to MP3s, to iTunes, and now streaming. Music streaming apps, such as Spotify, Apple Music, and Napster, have changed the way we listen to and share our favorite music.

As a digital streaming service, Spotify provides listeners with access to millions of sound recordings, podcasts, and videos. Listeners can search by artist, album, and genre, collaborate on playlists and share music with friends and other listeners. Spotify started in Sweden with a rights-managed model that protects the legal rights of artists, record labels, and media companies. It does an exceptional job of curating music for individual users' personal tastes, while connecting users to communities of listeners with similar musical interests. If you like electronic dance music or hip-hop, or any subgenre of these styles, you can follow a community of people who inform one another of the latest sounds and trends.

Spotify has built its following in a very powerful way by making recommendations based on individual listening behavior. If a listener keeps clicking on Top 40 day after day, the app will start recommending Top 40 selections from around the world. With a hundred million active users, of which forty million are paying subscribers, Spotify offers significant giveback to the artists it plays. For a nominal monthly fee, users can listen to any song they want by any artist, including B-side music and more obscure recordings and jams they wouldn't normally have access to. Depending on the time of day, the app will recommend suitable styles, such as lounging music for having coffee with friends, or girls' night party music because it's Friday night. Open the app on a Thursday and Throwback Thursday selections are available to boost listener energy.

Spotify and other streaming entertainment services such as Netflix build algorithms that actively engage with users. They use software codes written specifically to learn from user experience and give back to the individual in a way that suits personal tastes. This feature of today's apps differs significantly from software of the past. Earlier codes were written for a specific purpose, and that was it. Applications today are meeting consumer tastes and needs with software tailored to the local environment of individuals and communities.

GETTING DISRUPTIVE

Applications are typically cheap to produce. That's why there are so many of them out there. Some don't get very far, but the successful ones wind up going mainstream because they push the status quo. Apps can be disruptive in the marketplace and supplant existing industries. When a new app strikes a chord with individuals and communities at the local level, it is quickly adopted and can change the way things are done. Such was the case with the ride service Uber.

Uber took the time-tested tradition of waiting for taxicabs and turned it on its head with a mobile software application that connects drivers to customers who need a ride. In an industry where payments are usually in cash, Uber introduced digital payments that streamline the payment interaction between driver and rider. It's a very powerful tool. Uber has pushed its model to sixty-six countries and more than five hundred cities by appealing to digitally savvy people with mobile devices who want downloadable rides, convenience, and speed.

Uber succeeds by tracking the individual to know their behavior and to serve them better. The company uses its software to match consumer need with service. Aggregate data will steer drivers to crowded neighborhoods on a Saturday night. It's a powerful example of going local.

Now Uber is extending its concept of immediacy to other industries, such as food.

Uber Eats is a convenient restaurant takeout app that meets all the logistics of food ordering and delivery. For most people, the logistics of getting something done is the biggest hurdle. Uber Eats makes it easy to choose a restaurant, make an order, and receive delivery in record time. Companies like Uber that can push logistics to meet customer need with a convenient app are disrupting the way the game is played.

Stock investment and trading is another industry in disruption by AI. Trading floor investing by old-style brokerage houses has been supplanted in part by online discount firms such as E-Trade that facilitate electronic trading by individual investors. The next wave in investing is automated or robo-investing, which further empowers the investor.

The Canadian company Wealthsimple uses algorithms instead of people to manage investor money according to individual investment styles. Wealthsimple performs according to individual investor profiles. It invests on autopilot. Its algorithms put money where the indexes are by leveraging the S&P 500 and NASDAQ to make investing incredibly simple.

In just two years since coming on the scene, Wealthsimple already has upward of $600 million in assets under management. The company has taken the cut-rate brokerage mentality to the next step in a manner that outperforms the usual standards for electronic trading. It affords investors portfolio management without the fees associated with financial advisors. Robo-investing is an example of how disruptive technology is increasingly putting the individual first.

WORKING IT OUT

The IoT is driving innovation in the field of exercise and fitness. Limits on people's time have led to shorter workouts with cardio benefits and the concept of the "seven-minute workout." More recently, the seven-minute workout has become a feature of new software. An individual can now download a workout program and get a fairly intensive body workout that reaches all the important body groups. Workout apps provide feedback based on a person's exercise patterns, while keeping track of calories burned and assisting in scheduling workouts at appropriate intervals.

Seven-minute workouts have been linked to mobile devices such as the Apple Watch and integrated into Fitbit's wearable activity trackers. Fitness software has become a part of daily workout routines, sending users reminders about when to work out, which exercises to perform, and which muscle groups to focus on. Fitness programs monitor personal metrics related to performance, including calorie counting, heart-rate monitoring, and steps walked.

These new workout programs are a prime example of the IoT. Software embedded in wearable and handheld devices enable immediate connectivity and exchange of data. As the IoT becomes more a part of our everyday devices, we'll find daily activities easier to perform across our own personalized networks. In seven minutes, a person is assisted in burning off calories and boosting their metabolism. What could be better?

Fitness applications are also building fitness communities. The tracking device called Seven brings people together in seven-minute virtual workout sessions. People pace themselves with others over the course of days and weeks. The app also records personal milestones that help individuals engage more deeply in their own progress, tailoring workouts like a personal trainer.

Athletic shoe companies such as Under Armour and Asics have introduced smart running shoes that collect data via sensors embedded in the shoes themselves. Runners feed data into an application after each run to determine distance, time, and pace, tracking their progress and setting goals. The software provides infographs that depict performance and crunch data to forecast future performance.

The next stage of mobile running apps capitalizes on the IoT. AI is expanding to make transmission to wearable devices more immediate. Data collected by a wearer's shoe will upload to other wearables such as Fitbit in a further expansion of the IoT.

COLLABORATIVE SLACK

Slack, the cloud-based collaboration app, facilitates close-knit online communities. As a digital community platform, Slack affords live, secure messaging and sharing among invited participants. Topics or projects can be business based or simply interest based, such as people talking about fantasy football. Slack is the mechanism that gets folks talking, sharing, and collaborating.

The Slack app is integrated into larger ecosystems, including Google Drive, Dropbox, GitHub, Runscope, and ZenDesk. As a direct messaging tool, Slack allows people to communicate without use of email or SMS. It fills a niche need of both individuals and communities.

MOBILE REWARDS

The pharmacy chain Shoppers Drug Mart is the CVS of

Canada. Some years ago, the company started a customer loyalty program called Optimum. It's a hugely popular rewards program that recently launched a mobile rewards app that's best in class. Optimum is an intelligent, consumer-driven product that customers use to keep track of items that interest them.

The app also keeps track of individual spending habits, informing users of when items they favor go on sale. The application's algorithms are programmed to ping customers about merchandise, based on personal buying habits. It's a powerful tool that takes marketing to the individual level. Optimum knows each product and how long it lasts before a customer needs to make the next purchase.

This ability to curate purchasing patterns extends past the earlier functions of plastic loyalty cards. The application can generate shopping lists relevant to individual moms, seniors, or students. Optimum collects data and advises users on products according to relevancy but without heavy marketing. It entertains users with games for scoring points and winning cash for purchases. It's a great driver of sales and keeps Shoppers Drug Mart, which is a brick-and-mortar chain, competitive in an increasingly online marketplace.

CUSTOMIZING THE FUTURE

The local movement is driven by making the individual and the community central. AI allows businesses and product developers to cater to consumer needs. Applications, products, and services were previously built for the masses. Now they are customized for the individual, and the individual is the epicenter.

In the foreseeable future, AI will have a threefold impact:

First, traditional retailers will have better applications to garner information that helps them curate products around both the individual and the community.

Second, there will be more innovation in the realm of communication and collaboration.

Third, AI will increasingly connect ecosystems and data points in the IoT.

For example, people spend a lot of time in their cars, and voice-activated commands are already being used to control car entertainment systems, GPS, and mobile phones. In the future, we'll be seeing much more integration of mainstream apps in the automobile as well as the home. In the past few years, consumers have been getting a taste of what this integration will be like.

Amazon's Echo is an IoT, voice-controlled device for the home that connects to the Alexa app for news, music, weather reports, sports scores, and more. Meanwhile, Apple devices are equipped with the intelligent assistant Siri, an application that takes voice commands and can adapt to individual user voice patterns and search preferences. And Microsoft's Cortana, another personal assistant software, takes voice commands and answers user questions by accessing the Bing search engine.

We'll be seeing more of these and other applications plugged into cars, homes, and offices. Microsoft, Apple, Google, and others will continue to innovate in the vast arena of the IoT as interconnected technologies become mainstream. Machine learning and software will be interacting more and more in our day-to-day lives, and apps will be accessed on the go for navigation, shopping lists, and information gathering, all curated for the individual.

The future of home building is also being changed by the IoT. Homeowners will have sensors in each room and more intelligent thermostats for heating and cooling systems. Intelligent devices such as Google's Nest will act as a central hub, controlling the home environment and saving the homeowner on energy costs.

Over the next three to five years, technicians will need to be equipped to service increasingly intelligent home environments. As a person returns home from work, software in their car will be communicating with software in their home and making adjustments. Our devices will be wired like digital nervous systems tailored to individual lifestyles. Changes in software interconnectedness are the driving forces with the consumer at the center. Industries will require new skillsets to meet these changes on the near horizon.

HOW TO JOIN THE AI REVOLUTION

AI shapes how individuals connect with products and services. It drives connectivity and enables the IoT. AI and the IoT are the growth engines of the new global economy. Companies that understand and integrate IT and AI are better able to reach their customers and bring the point of sale closer to individuals and communities.

AI makes it easier for companies to know their customers and easier for customers to select and buy products. Software applications are at the heart of localmotion because they empower people to work and communicate, while also empowering businesses to reach larger markets. Apps expand opportunities at the local level by empowering connectivity. They can be produced cheaply and disrupt the marketplace at the local level before going mainstream to reach wider communities of users.

AI that tracks and aggregates data is changing the face of industries from transportation to stock investment. Applications provide for portfolio management and programmed fitness and health, all putting the individual first. Algorithms help sellers keep track of individual spending habits and ping customers about merchandise based on their personal tastes.

This ability to curate purchasing patterns allows for relevancy without heavy marketing. It makes the individual central.

Advertising is for the masses, but AI customizes for the individual within a community. Products such as voice-controlled devices for the home, intelligent heating and cooling systems, and devices and software for machine learning are increasingly shaping our lives. Innovation in software interconnectedness and machine learning will continue to drive industry and the marketplace into the future.

Chapter 9

SENTIMENT ANALYSIS

Sentiment analysis is the concept of analyzing how a customer feels or communicates about a brand. Companies collect many different data points to help them understand customer preference and behavior. Until now, companies relied on marketing to the mainstream, the masses, but this is no longer the case. The individual is the new focal point.

Companies are using complex, data-processing applications to capture, curate, and analyze "big data." In this way, they extract value from aggregated data and use predictive, behavioral analytics to gauge consumer sentiment, opinion, and preference.

Big data is the gold mine of marketing. The goal for any new product or service is to understand how customers are thinking, feeling, communicating, and behaving.

The challenge of marketers is to figure this all out. So much data is out there, but until now, it hasn't all been used. Companies from big banks to candy bar companies and retailers from Walmart to Amazon are now better equipped with software applications for social media analysis to more deeply understand potential customers.

Unlike apps, which are driven from the bottom-up by consumers who adopt apps at the ground level, big data analysis is driven from the top down by companies that collect data points on their customers. Starbucks and McDonald's use Wi-Fi not only to provide web-connected service for customers but also to mine customer data. They use data gathered on foot traffic to build algorithms that tell them, for instance, that of the ten thousand people who walked by a store location, 2 percent actually came in.

TRACKING CUSTOMER SENTIMENT

An early adopter of sentiment analysis is HootSuite, the social media management platform. The company began tracking Facebook, LinkedIn, and Twitter posts and developed a model for selling its service to companies that need to understand customer sentiment about their brands. HootSuite went to companies such as Coca-Cola and Intel and said, "We can actually give you the tools to analyze what consumers are saying on social media about your products."

A slew of large corporations use Hootsuite to track people's feelings toward their brands. The software enables companies to intercept data in real time. Hootsuite helps businesses build relevancy by conducting sentiment analysis and conveying that information so that businesses can jump on the conversation very quickly.

Sentiment analysis is marketing research on steroids. Traditional marketing research uses field studies, focus groups, and surveys, but it's passive. In the new world of marketing, sentiment analysis takes place in real time. Using Hootsuite's social media management platform, Coca-Cola can know that there are, let's say, 1,500 people talking about Coke at a given moment on X number of channels, in X regions and geography. This kind of data is immediately relevant and actionable, increasing the opportunities and pathways for Coke to engage with its customers.

Customer sentiment is also applicable in an industry such as banking. Barclays Bank in the UK has a mobile application called Pingit, which is used for one-to-one money transfers. Ten percent of Barclays's twenty million customers, or two million people, use Pingit. When Barclays first launched the Pingit product, it got customer backlash. There was negativity around the product's usability. To deal with the issues, the bank used sentiment analysis in real time on social media to find out exactly what customers didn't like about its product. It needed to know which facets of the app functioned well and which didn't make sense or were difficult to use. By doing sentiment analysis in real time, the company was able to make the changes to enhance its product. Barclays honed Pingit to the point that it's now the dominant player in the UK for transferring money using mobile phones.

Corporations that launch products without adequate sentiment analysis are just slowing down the works. It's a waste of time and money to introduce a product, wait for consumer reviews to come in, then launch a new update of a better version. Companies that use sentiment analysis from the start are making products that are much more valuable to their customers.

REACHING INDIVIDUALS

Walmart is a company that's done extremely well in sentiment analysis. It has its own software application called Polaris that was built in-house. Polaris does sentiment analysis on the many different combinations and permutations of how people do online searches. The application analyzes what potential customers are searching for and how they phrase their searches.

What Walmart has done is to integrate data gathering and tracking in order to spot consumer patterns around the globe. The company uses sentiment analysis to see what journalists are saying about its products. Walmart also tests new products on social media to gauge public reaction. The chain has about 300,000 social media mentions a week and about a million customer data points every hour. That's a whole lot of data to sift through, and Walmart shares those data sets with Hootsuite for further analysis.

Walmart's approach to sentiment analysis is holistic. There are about one hundred million keywords out there, and the company is constantly bidding against the Amazons of the world and the many smaller and medium-sized companies. Walmart also redesigned and customized its website to specific regions in order to reflect local sentiment. It's an example of how companies are localizing the relevancy of product offerings based on algorithms. Buying habits change from region to region, Quebec to California, and further afield across languages and geography.

The next step for Walmart is to deepen its relationship to the individual. The next generation of sentiment analysis will enable frontline retailers to receive specific customer data from a company's social media and PR teams. A sales clerk with a mobile phone would get information in real time about the product preferences of a customer who just walked into the store. When a customer enters a Walmart store, that person's purchasing track record and search history will be available on their mobile phone app. The store will know which products and special offers best suit that customer. This is called geofencing, creating a digital perimeter around a store that enables it to geo-target individual customer needs. When the customer enters the store, Walmart would push offers and discounts tailored to that person.

Personalization is where localmotion is going. There are ten million users of Hootsuite around the world, including MailChimp, the email marketing application. The next step is to bring data to the microlevel at the point of sale. Giving sales clerks actionable data is crucial, because they need to know who the customer in front of them is. A clothing salesperson would actually have a profile of a repeat customer and engage that customer on a new sale item. Grocery stores will become more acutely aware of individual customer sentiment. Upon entering the store, an individual's profile preferences will be linked to previous shopping trips through mobile applications.

We're at the threshold of aggregated data reaching front-line salespeople. Until now, big data has been informing marketing people and product developers in the corporate suites. These folks have been tapping into sentiment analysis at the macrolevel, gaining a deeper understanding of consumer sentiment to use in marketing and product development. Hootsuite engages companies at the macrolevel, but the next wave of sentiment analysis will be heading toward deeper personalization.

The backbone of this capacity is using social media to create algorithms for machine learning. This goes far beyond human beings sitting around monitoring chatter about Walmart on hundreds of different social media networks. Machine learning is much faster and getting faster all the time, as automated functions are increasingly spitting out relevant information to companies.

Sentiment analysis is a hub that connects to different channels, which include the software application that gathers the data, the business that uses it, and the social media from which data is gathered. Companies that know how to use big data and algorithms applied to individuals will be the ones that succeed.

PERSONALIZED YIELD MANAGEMENT

Yield management is an old-school economics term related to supply and demand. The greater the supply and the lower the demand for a product, the cheaper the selling price. When supply is low but demand is high, the higher the selling price. A company will therefore manage its yield on a product based on supply and demand. Yield management looks at how a company creates the right amount of product elasticity.

People who sell art do a pretty good job of this. The first art prints to sell of a limited run of lithographs will likely sell for less. But as the quantity dwindles, the remaining pieces will sell for more. Of course the value will be highest when all the prints are sold out. That's when a print owner can resell a print at an even higher price.

Airlines do extremely well using yield management. They figured out that when there are only two seats left on a flight, those are going to be two very expensive seats. The closer to a fly date that seats are booked, the more expensive the seats. Certain days of the week are more desirable and therefore more expensive to fly. Other industries are learning from this playbook.

Movie theaters typically set their prices based on adult, child, or senior citizen. But it's likely that they'll be changing to a yield management pricing model, discounting tickets at off times when business is slow. On warm, sunny days when people are more likely to be outdoors, theaters can draw customers with ticket discounts. On rainy days, tickets would be more likely to sell at a premium.

With the advent of sentiment analysis based on big data, retailers are better positioned to use real-time pricing and yield management according to algorithms and machine learning. For example, Macy's website automatically adjusts pricing on more than seventy-three million products in real time. The company does it based on inventory and demand. In addition to sentiment analysis based on information gathering on social media, Macy's is using its software platform and machine learning to ascertain what customers are buying online in real time. The company then links the two information sources together for a more complete picture of purchasing behaviors and adjusts prices accordingly.

Walmart is also linking sentiment analysis of social media with searches on its website. By aggregating the data and adjusting prices in real time, the retailer has improved online shoppers' completed purchases by 10 to 15 percent. The significance to Walmart is in the billions of dollars. The chain will continue to do this as it gears up for conducting sentiment analysis down to the individual level. The website is in further development for tracking and gathering data on individual buying choices and patterns. As mentioned earlier, Walmart already tailors its website to regional buyers. It will also be personalizing and curating website offerings to individual customers, and the payoff will be an even bigger bang for the buck.

PERSONALIZED MEDICINE

Supercomputers are at various stages of deployment in health care at the patient level to crunch data points on individuals. Computers such as IBM's Watson are capable of conducting analysis of patient data to assist in treatment plans and emergency medicine. Data analysis at this level will speed treatment by shortening time for blood reports, lab results, CT scans, and critical interventions. The future of personalized medicine is unfolding.

Right now in the United States, 80 percent of health data is invisible to the current system because it's unstructured and fragmented. Both IBM and Intel are vying for this health-care space, developing products designed for diagnosis and treatment at the individual level. Supercomputers are using the cloud and smart data from different points to provide analytics. Part of Intel's mission is to connect lab machinery in a manner to extract and correlate information. Intel's microchips will pool information from different sources to speed health-care delivery. It will synchronize data on individuals to match treatment and diagnoses for clinical decisions.

Intelligent computing will transform health care at both the micro- and the macrolevels by obtaining and analyzing data much more quickly and tailoring it to individual diagnosis and treatment. In hospitals, various machines push out different pieces of information. Providers have to interpret and apply data to each individual case. The assistance of supercomputers in crunching data, recognizing regional macrotrends, and applying data to cases at the microlevel, will speed treatment and boost positive results. Watson can figure out trends very quickly on a regional level, while Intel's chips, because they are ingrained in many different machines, can synchronize at the patient level.

Predictive clinical analytics is vital to personalized medicine because each patient is unique. Intelligent computing is on a quest for data gathering to assist in transforming health care. It's a corollary to how companies collect many different data points to help them understand customer preference and behavior. The individual is increasingly the focal point.

PERSONALIZED TRAINING DATA

The sports apparel brand Under Armour also works with IBM's Watson. The company uses Watson to aggregate data from the company's own app called Record, as well as third-party data and research on fitness, nutrition, and lifestyle. The result is training plans curated to specific individuals. For instance, a thirty-two-year-old woman who is training for a 5K race can use Under Armour's app to plan a training regimen suited to her distinct needs down to the particulars of diet, running routes, workout frequency, and progression of training.

Under Armour is enabling individuals and changing the expectations for what's possible in the realm of athletic training. It's far more personalized than the usual generic training app. Through extremely fast and robust data collection and analysis, IBM's Watson is helping companies like Under Armour serve the individual. Under Armour probably spent quite a bit of cash to develop this program, so the price of entry to this level of sentiment analysis is not cheap. The upshot is, however, that the company is building customer loyalty for its apparel.

Other traditional sports apparel brands, the likes of Adidas and Nike, have not gone to this level of data collection and analysis. With Under Armour spending tons of money in this direction, the race for the local individual is on. It's a significant shift in the way big corporations are thinking of the individual. This is the competition at the center of localmotion.

VISIBILITY IN THE NEW MARKETPLACE

Companies that don't pay close attention to the role that big data and sentiment analysis play for the individual and community in the new marketplace will be left behind in a big way. Whether a business is a retailer, a bank, a restaurant chain, or an online store, it will need to understand data to offer relevant products and services that customers need and want, and in the manner and time frame customers require. Businesses will need to respond in real time and strike while the iron is hot.

Sentiment analysis as it has played out over the last several years is a fairly new industry. It's new because social media is new. Big data has been gathering hordes of information for a while now, but what's new is how quickly information is analyzed and acted upon by smart companies. With social media management platforms like Hootsuite, companies can access sentiment analysis, understand their customers, and respond in real time.

Organizations that learn from data and sentiment analysis and improve products and services to meet customer need will thrive. They will be the ones that include their customers in new product development. These are the companies that will rise on customer loyalty and be most visible in the marketplace.

HOW TO USE SENTIMENT ANALYSIS
TO KNOW CUSTOMERS

The challenge for companies is to understand their customers. The success of any new product or service requires that companies gather, curate, and analyze data to know and interpret customer preference and behavior in the marketplace. Sentiment analysis is this process of studying and evaluating data to gauge customer opinion and predict behavior.

Companies use social media management platforms to track people's feelings toward their brands. By intercepting data in real time, companies can respond quickly to customer sentiment expressed on social media. Companies that integrate data gathering and tracking can test new products on social media and weigh public reaction. They can customize their social media and website management platforms to specific regions to reflect local sentiment. In this way, they can localize the relevance of their products and deepen their relationship to the individual and community.

Traditional marketing methods such as surveys and focus groups are more passive. Sentiment analysis in real time is immediately actionable and opens more opportunities to engage customers. It allows companies to more quickly and effectively respond to customer feedback and make changes to enhance a product or service. In our fast-paced marketplace, the older methods of launch and long lag times for product updates leave customers in the lurch. Sentiment analysis cuts to the chase by opening pathways to quick response.

Machine learning is getting faster. Automated functions are speeding real-time pricing and inventory management. Sentiment analysis is at the threshold of aggregating data from frontline salespeople. Product offerings on websites are being tailored to regional buyers. With sentiment analysis, the individual and community are increasingly the focal point of our localmotion marketplace.

CONCLUSION

When online retailer Amazon announced in June 2017 that it would purchase Whole Foods for $13.7 billion, the world stood up and listened. Why would a company lauded as the leading-edge online retailer purchase a brick-and-mortar food brand?

Amazon's vision is to marry the best in personalized online retail with the best in localized community retail and bridge the gap in food sales. Online grocery retail has fallen short of expectations as customers have shown a preference for community-based grocers. Localmotion is all about getting nearer to the customer, both conceptually and, wherever possible, physically. Amazon recognizes that Whole Foods has established a brand that cares about local food and local producers. Acquiring Whole Foods will help put a more human face on Amazon.

At the same time, Whole Foods' 465 physical stores will become an addition and extension of Amazon's distribution centers, providing greater opportunities for order fulfillment and customer order pickup. While a customer is shopping at Whole Foods and getting in-store discounts with their Amazon Prime membership, they could go ahead and put an Amazon order together on the spot. Amazon also expects to boost its online grocery sales and deliveries of nonperishable, packaged foods. In so doing, Amazon will be giving the Krogers of the world a run for their food money.

Amazon has also announced plans for a mobile-checkout food store in Seattle and is opening bookstores in major American cities. Along with its new Prime Now hour-or-less delivery services, the company is bringing more of its operations to the local level. Amazon knows that customers want diversity and choice. The company has spent years refining its understanding of consumer habits and curating its online marketplace to meet customer needs. Amazon's wealth of data gathering and analysis will be applied to its Whole Foods venture to further refine purchasing and delivery.

AI AND THE IOT

As we discussed earlier, industries go through three phases. Phase one is marketing to the masses as exemplified by

Henry Ford's automobile assembly lines. In phase two, a company strives to meet more individualized tastes, such as Starbucks offering select roasts and handcrafted coffee to the North American market. In phase three, products are more personalized. I call this phase "deep local." It's the *Cheers* model, kind of like the old, corner bar where "everyone knows your name."

Phase three companies are seeking to meet personal consumer needs. Up-and-coming consumers—millennials and Gen Z—no longer want to spend precious time behind the wheel of a car or contribute to global warming by burning fossil fuels. In phase three, innovative auto companies such as Tesla are disrupting the auto industry with electric-powered, self-driving vehicles that have the potential to free the consumer from traditional constraints. Autonomous vehicles will be programmed to meet individual needs, driving habits, road conditions, and destinations.

AI and robotics are cycling through the phases. The first phase involved only simple assembly line tasks, which gave way to more complexity in phase two. As this complexity increases, we'll be experiencing more sophisticated interaction and communication among machines in the third phase.

For example, mobile phones are increasingly a phase

three industry. Smartphones allow individuals to download whatever they want, listen to whatever they want, and do whatever they want at any moment in time. They are extensions of ourselves in an increasingly connected world. Apple's personal assistant, Siri, can figure out your patterns of driving and tell you the best routes to take from point A to points B, C, and D as it navigates your commute home with all the stops you need to make along the way.

Networks of software-embedded objects that enable connectivity and the collection and exchange of data—what we call the IoT—are empowering our lives. AI is bridging our physical and digital touch points, from the internet to transportation, to devices in our homes.

We are experiencing only the first generation of the IoT. The vast majority of people don't yet have a Nest thermostat, Fitbit, or Google Home. There's still a lot of catching up to do. Industry is still targeting early adopters. The future will involve crossing the chasm of mass adoption, and it will require an entire ecosystem of connected devices, individuals, and communities.

We'll be seeing changes in all industries. The IoT will be generating the kind of connected intelligence and communication that serves to reduce workplace injury and improve quality control. It will increase efficiency with robotic devices checking retail store shelves and automatically ordering stock from distribution centers. Adoption of connected networks will occur sooner in B2B industries and spread to the masses from there. But in a connected world, the individual is king. Industry growth hinges on understanding individual needs at the local level and meeting those needs. Individual consumers have become the driving force of industry decision making.

Our smartphones are mobile digital computers that are personalizing our world. AI will increasingly propel what we buy, how we save and invest, where we recreate, and how we work. Our autonomous vehicles will be alerting our home thermostats to make temperature adjustments in advance of arriving home. At the center of this localmotion are individuals and communities.

TRANSFORMING BUYING AND SELLING

Nothing says "I love you" better than flowers, and no company is better prepared to help you say it than 1-800-Flowers.com. The online company wants to be your personal assistant and help you get your message out. The assistant is called GWYN (Gifts When You Need). GWYN is an AI concierge powered by IBM Watson's Fluid Expert Personal Shopper (XPS) software platform. GWYN interacts with customers using natural language while learning customer preferences. At 1-800-Flowers.com, GWYN dialogues with customers to determine the specific gift occasion, the gift recipient and relationship, personal tastes, and all the details necessary to help the customer choose the perfect gift.

Another company that utilizes Watson's personal concierge software is North Face, the outdoor equipment retailer. North Face launched its interactive online shopping experience to more deeply engage its customers in online buying. The dialogue-based recommendation engine uses natural conversation to help customers discover and refine their product selection. A customer might enter details such as "I need a jacket for light hiking." In turn, the concierge will ask, "Where are you going?" "In what season?" "Are you male or female?" Watson will crunch the data and the concierge will make specific outerwear recommendations.

In this manner, advanced search tools are applying AI to transform the retail experience. It's the kind of smart search functionality that will make or break companies in an increasingly competitive digitized and localized marketplace. Sellers need to take customers down a purchase funnel to make sure they buy a product. They do this by reducing the anonymity of a purchase.

As mentioned in chapter 8, AI is outperforming the usual standards for electronic trading. The robo-investment advising company Wealthsimple uses algorithms to put money where the indexes are by leveraging the S&P 500 and NASDAQ to make investing incredibly simple. Robo-advising is shaking up the financial investment industry.

Every industry is being shaken up and companies need to grasp these facts. Reaching buyers has moved past advertising and in-store promotions. Marketing can no longer be passive. Even as sellers shift to social media, they can't rely on Facebook or Twitter to simply capture attention. Companies need to actively build community and create customer experience. Buying is increasingly about relationships.

As described in chapter 7, PepsiCo's social media campaign for Mountain Dew fostered ongoing interactions by soliciting suggestions for new bottle designs and new flavors. It was all about creating a new culture around Mountain Dew that didn't involve traditional advertising. Consumers interacted with the company and with one another as well, building community around the product through participation and creativity. The campaign made the product more relevant to millennials and expanded the dialogue to a wider fan base.

The takeaway for companies is to get out of the passive role by constantly engaging potential buyers. In our new world of localmotion, consumers themselves become salespeople.

Nothing is more frustrating to consumers than long waits on the phone for customer service. This is why millennials want nothing to do with it, and why smart companies are shifting to robots called chatbots. Using the same AI and software platform as digital concierges, customer service chatbots curate products and make recommendations to customers. This is why mobile phone companies such as Verizon and travel brands such as Kayak and Expedia are investing in chatbots.

It's why Sephora, the beauty product brand, used "bot" software to conduct its most recent customer survey. What's remarkable is that the survey had a 40 percent completion rate, which is way higher than traditional survey response. Behind the record response are millennials who are already using WeChat, WhatsApp, and Facebook Messenger for chatting with friends.

Traditional customer service is structured around customer service reps who are trained to answer frequently asked questions. Such frontline customer service is intensive and expensive, which is why so many companies have offshored these operations to countries like India where labor is cheaper. But wait times are problematic, and customers on hold are never happy.

Chatbots are the solution for changing the face of customer

service. Interactive, AI bots can dialogue with customers and steer them to solutions and informed purchases more quickly and effectively than overworked reps. Millennial customers aren't put off by chatbots and are, in fact, freer in expressing personal preferences to an anonymous bot. When a bot asks, "What are you interested in?" it doesn't feel quite so invasive as a human being asking the same question. And it sure beats waiting on hold for the next available member of a customer service team.

AUTHENTICITY, INDIVIDUAL, AND COMMUNITY

In these rapidly changing times, companies are under increasing pressure to meet the needs of individuals and communities. As I mentioned in the introduction, the global marketplace is at a tipping point.

In its acquisition of Whole Foods, Amazon is setting a high bar for the integration of online and local store sales. Savvy companies know that sales today are all about personalization, customization, data crunching, and curating for the individual. Smart sellers are learning to leverage every interaction with the customer.

The evolution to localmotion is happening globally and locally. Our younger cohorts of millennials and Gen Z are tuned in digitally and know no other way of doing business. They are digital natives with new reference points for how they want to live, buy, and consume. Marketers can no longer rely on segmenting populations by age or gender. Instead, they are linking and refining data collection to the individual and courting authenticity.

Authenticity, the quality of being genuine, carries more weight in the marketplace than ever before. It increasingly determines whom we associate with, what and how we consume, and where we invest. For consumers today, the value of commodities is increasingly linked to the greater good. Honesty and integrity carry more weight in a global society of individuals who find value in community.

We are still at the dawn of the mobile digital age. In defining localmotion at this moment in time, I've endeavored to take a moving snapshot of an evolving marketplace in flux. Change happens rapidly but also in fits and starts as technology builds upon itself.

This book, therefore, is a beginning. *Localmotion* was conceived as a tour of the new global marketplace in the second decade of the twenty-first century. We've seen how the consumer landscape has been localized to the individual and the community. We've seen how business is harnessing technology to better understand and reach people.

As I said at the beginning, localmotion has caught on

because it's where people want to go. I hope to continue the tour and track the many changes as they happen. I invite you to come along with me at my blog www.LocalMotionToday.com.

Innovation is inevitable, and I, among many, want to be out front catching the next wave. I expect you do, too.

ABOUT THE AUTHOR

 **ALEX BARSEGHIAN** is the group vice president of sales and marketing for United States retail at Blackhawk Network. He is responsible for driving over $15 billion in revenue for products and services through retail and digital channels. Previously, he headed Original Content for Blackhawk, where he was in charge of new products, as well as successfully launching Happy Cards in over 50,000 retail locations. In 2008, he founded Samba Connects, which became the fastest growing company in the United Kingdom and was a top 50 fastest growing company in Canada two years in a row prior to its acquisition by Blackhawk in 2016. He has held various senior positions at Aeroplan, Royal LePage, and MDS International. An entrepreneur at heart, Barseghian thrives at scaling products and companies by simplifying and operationalizing complex problems.